HOW DO YOU WORK ◄THIS► LIFE THING?

ADVICE FOR THE NEWLY INDEPENDENT ON ROOMMATES, JOBS, SEX,

EVERYTHING
THAT COUNTS

LIZZIE POST

HOW DO YOU WORK ◄THIS► LIFE THING?

Collins
An Imprint of HarperCollinsPublishers

HarperCollins books may be purchased for educational, business, or sales promotional use. For information please write: Special Markets Department, HarperCollins Publishers, 10 East 53rd Street, New York, NY 10022.

FIRST EDITION

Designed by Judith Stagnitto Abbate/Abbate Design

Library of Congress Cataloging-in-Publication Data has been applied for.

ISBN-10: 0-06-082375-5
978-0-06-082375-7

07 08 09 10 11 WBC/RRD 10 9 8 7 6 5 4 3 2 1

For years you have been my idol, from your artwork to knowing everything about hockey to digging clams with your toes. When you asked me to write this book, I felt how much you believe in me. It was always there before, but throughout the three years I've been working on this project I have seen and felt how supportive and proud you are of me—not just with my writing, but with my life. This book is for you, for always giving me opportunity and love. I love you, Dad.

ACKNOWLEDGMENTS

THIS BOOK COULD NEVER HAVE come to print without the help of so many people. I'd like to thank Royce Flippin for all of the long hours he has spent making sure my blunt comedic writing was Emily Post-worthy, as well as his wife, Alexis, whose thoughts and suggestions appear frequently in the text. I couldn't have asked for two cooler editors—you both really understand the twenty-something's perspective. I'd also like to thank Toni Sciarra for her endless efforts to broaden the book's demographic, and in bridging the gap between writer and publisher. In addition, I'd like to thank Mary Ellen O'Neill, who came into this project and spent serious time getting to know the etiquette of the Newly Independent—and me. Katherine Cowles, my agent, also deserves a very large thank you for all of her time and effort, from reading manuscript pages to finding a future for me. She is far more than an agent to our institute.

To my family and coworkers at the Emily Post Institute, especially my parents, Tricia and Peter, my Aunt Cindy, and Elizabeth Howell, who have all worked so hard to help me through my first book: thank you for all your advice and support. To my sister Anna, for being my first roommate and for paving the way: thank you, Lila Jo—I've learned so very much from you.

The roommates deserve a very large thank you (and possibly medals for putting up with me). Sophie, we made it work, from DOA3 and "What Ales," to leftovers and movies—we taught each other a lot. Christina, you so patiently taught me so much about myself, and I've never felt like you moved away. Trevor, thank you so much for everything: from a home on the weekends to living in California, you brought so very much to my life. And finally, their names occur rarely in the book, but they are the two friends who have been there for me throughout it all: Claudia and Estelle, I am truly privileged to have you both in my life and my heart.

CONTENTS

INTRODUCTION

WHY This BOOK?

L IVING ON YOUR OWN is all about being free, right? Free from living at home with parental figures, free from dealing with siblings and daily chores, free to make your own hours and do your own thing. You're completely liberated, answerable to no one—until you start running into comments like these:

"My roommate leaves her clothes all over the place!"

"I loaned my friend fifty bucks, and I don't know when he'll pay me back."

"It's two in the morning, and the next-door neighbors are still partying on their porch!"

"That's the third night in a row that Tom's friend has crashed on our couch. Someone needs to say something. . . ."

When you're living in your own place, whether it's a dorm room, an apartment, or a shared house, it's tempting to think that anything goes. But the truth of the matter is this: Now that you're living on your own, what you do and how you interact with other people matters *more than ever*. Because now you're building your own world, your own relationships, and your own future—and your success depends completely on how you choose to handle both yourself and the other people in your life.

That's where this book comes in. In all areas of life, the newly independent faces big challenges. And frankly, we aren't going to get it right all the time. But even in today's casual, comfortable world—where what's mine is yours, replacement of ruined things is rare, and the drunken excuse is all too common—there is still a time-tested tool we can use to guide us:

Etiquette.

Yes, I said *etiquette*. No, not the way you think of it: rules, manners, old farts pontificating on stuffy, out-of-date customs. I'm talking about *real* etiquette—the attitudes and actions that can actually mean the difference between success and failure for you in your relationships with your friends, significant others, professors, employers, and, yes, even your parents. It's the etiquette that my great-great-grandmother Emily Post truly believed in.

Emily said: "Whenever two people come together and interact, you have etiquette." That's it: no rules, no fuss over place settings—just awareness of how you and your actions affect those around you. Used the right way, etiquette can turn every encounter you have with another person—your roommate, your landlord, your boyfriend or girlfriend, the store owner down the street—into a positive experience.

Best of all, learning how to use etiquette the right way is incredibly easy. All you need to do is remember that virtually every aspect of etiquette, from navigating a fancy dinner party to dividing up the household chores with your roommates, is grounded in three basic principles: *consideration, respect,* and *honesty.*

Consideration arises whenever we make a sincere effort to think about how a certain situation affects everyone involved. As we work to solve problems with roommates, friends, or coworkers, etiquette teaches us to consider the different points of view and varying perspectives of others as we try to figure out the best solution for everyone concerned. Consideration involves tact, diplomacy, and the ability to put yourself in someone else's place—in other words, empathy—to help you maneuver through life's sometimes thorny passages.

After you've exercised consideration, the principle of *respect* comes into play. Every action you make affects others positively or negatively. When you choose to act on a positive solution, you've chosen to act with respect. Acting with respect signals that you've decided to accept those around you exactly as they are. You don't have to like them, but you can still *choose* to respect them just as they are.

Finally, *honesty* is essential for good communication, which is the basis of all interactions. Without it, you can never be sure of what you are told. This principle isn't just about honesty with others; it's also about being honest with ourselves—the kind of honesty that allows us to recognize our own imperfections. Honesty with yourself kicks in with a feeling of relief and contentment (that feeling of "doing the right thing") when you've made a good choice, or guilt when you've chosen a wrong or disrespectful action.

Once you've mastered these three essential principles of etiquette, you'll have the tools to deal with virtually any situation in any setting. That's because etiquette is *not* about rigid rules or achieving an upper-crust social rank. Etiquette is a *philosophy* of how to handle your interactions with everyone you come across in life—boss, roommate, friend, or stranger.

How Do You Work This Life Thing? will show you how to put this philosophy into action. In the course of researching this book, the Emily Post Institute interviewed newly independents from many different backgrounds, asking them about difficulties they've encountered living on their own. This book reflects the real issues these and other newly independents face in the three major areas of daily life: when you're at home; when you're out in the world; and when you're at work or (if you're a student) in class. As you read these sections, you'll discover how to apply the basic tenets of etiquette in order to make *every aspect* of your life smoother and more fulfilling. And isn't that what living on your own is all about?

PART 1

HoMe SWeeT HoMe

CHAPTER 1

HOW TO AVOID KILLING YOUR ROOMMATE (AND OTHERS):

THE "THREE C'S" APPROACH TO BUILDING BETTER RELATIONSHIPS

Y OU MADE IT! You're finally living on your own—in your own space, pursuing your own lifestyle. Of course, being independent also means that you now have to deal with roommates, a landlord, friends, colleagues, professors, and other assorted acquaintances as you juggle job, home, and social life. And *that* means mastering the "three C's" of living with others: communication, compromise, and commitment. If you already understand these three key concepts completely, just put this book down and walk away.

Still here?

That's what I thought.

As the Introduction pointed out, consideration, respect, and honesty are the three core principles of good etiquette. The "three C's" let you put these principles into action. They're especially important when it comes to the people you share your home with. Being able to communicate and compromise on issues related to your living space is absolutely essential. As important as these household issues are, however, many people find it hard to talk about them. I hear it all the time from friends with roommates, and from my own mouth as well: "I just don't know how to raise the subject . . ."; "Can I really ask him that?"; "I don't want to seem like a nag . . ."

In general, roommates are scared to death of honest communication—yet it's one of the fundamental secrets of living with other people. Of course, communication eventually *does* happen. But after a week of pent-up anger, the words are rarely happy ones.

COMMUNICATING YOUR WAY TO PEACE

What good does it do to set household rules? Half the time my roommates just ignore them. Their attitude is basically, "So, sue me." I don't know how to communicate with them so that they take it seriously. HELP!

My former roommate Sophie and I came up with our own communications system when we first talked about living together, long before we actually moved in. Fresh out of the dorms, I had never been through the kind of major communication breakdowns that Sophie had experienced with other roommates. So Sophie, fed up with apartment drama, and I, a newcomer to roommate dilemmas, sat down and discussed how best to communicate with each other. When one of us was bothered by something or when the apartment situation was getting out of hand—be it messiness, noise, or overdue bills—how were we going to address the issue without offending each other?

Finally, we hit on the idea of approaching the other roommate with the words "We need to have a roommate talk." As I write these words now, they sound so lame—but I can't tell you how much this phrase did for us. It let each of us know that this was not a time to feel accused but rather a time to discuss the problem at hand. To help the conversation along, we both made a point of swallowing our pride and avoiding the urge to make excuses or become defensive or accusatory. (Sometimes a drink really helped, too.) Our talks were a time for looking at ourselves not as Sophie and Lizzie, two individuals with busy lives, but as two people who have a *responsibility to be good roommates to each other.*

For example, I realized that Sophie was short with me whenever I came home just after she'd cleaned the whole apartment. I finally sat down with her and told her that I felt bad—it seemed that every time the house got really messy, she'd wait to clean it on a day when I was out. I felt that before I had a chance to actually help with the cleaning, she would take it on herself to do it all—and then would be annoyed that *she* was the one cleaning up the big messes.

Sophie confessed that earlier that very day she'd been venting to a friend about the fact that she was always the one who cleaned up when the apartment was a big mess. And the friend had floated this theory: Maybe you're sitting around while Lizzie's away all day, getting

INSTANT TIP

If you run into problems in your home, everyone involved has a responsibility to talk it over and come up with a collective solution. The plan can be anything you want it to be, as long as all the roommates agree on it and it addresses the problem effectively: "We sat down together and made a deal about cleaning the apartment: I clean one room, my roommate cleans another."

stewed about the mess and her inability to clean it right then and there, and then you use that anger to clean the apartment before she gets home. That way, when Lizzie comes home, you can show her in a passive-aggressive way that "Hey, the apartment was a disaster, and *I* cleaned it *again!*"

We made an agreement: First, we'd both try hard to keep the apartment from turning into a disaster area, and second, when the house *did* become a mess, we'd either clean it together, or we'd each tackle half the work on our own time.

WAYS OF BRIDGING THE GAP

In this fashion, Sophie and I made an effort to keep the lines of communication open. Sometimes the effort ended well, and sometimes it didn't. That's life. What's important, though, is that we found a way to talk about the things that were bothering us. If you and your roomies want to live in peace and tranquility, you'll need to find your own ways of bringing up difficult topics.

For example, I had friends who lived in a six-bedroom house. Once a month, all the housemates held a meeting to discuss any problems that had been percolating. They developed a few easy strategies for making their system work. For starters, they chose a time when everyone could be there. This wasn't a "Hey, are you free Thursday evening?" type of thing. They made sure to schedule the meeting for an evening when no one had a class or a job conflict, and each housemate was then really good about keeping that night free.

My friends also created a system for coming up with meeting topics. They kept a dry-eraser board in the kitchen, and anyone who had an "apartment problem" would write their issue on the board. You'd

MEETING NIGHT

- Pick a night when everyone can make the meeting.
- Don't make other plans that night.
- Have a clear agenda.
- Create a system for speaking that gives everyone a chance to raise key issues.
- Restate all compromises clearly to make sure that everyone is on the same page.

see things like "DISHES!" or "FOOD" scrawled there. The agenda for each month's meeting would be the items listed on the board.

What really made these meetings work, one friend confided to me, was that no one made up excuses. If someone was being lazy about doing her share of the dishes, she didn't say, "Oh, but I've been so bogged down with my work this month . . ." Instead, she sucked it up and acknowledged that she hadn't been doing her job. No one could hide—and by the end of the meeting, everyone knew what had to be done to keep the problems from recurring.

Having said that, the one pitfall in this type of a system is the problem of the group sometimes ganging up on one person. One person may be the source of a certain problem—but this doesn't mean you need to make that person feel as if he or she is the source of *all* your household problems or is a bad person. The bottom line: Take care with your choice of words when pointing out where others have fallen short, even in a "house meeting" setting. Besides, if someone has already 'fessed up, there's no need to play the blame game—they already realize they've made a mistake.

FIVE WAYS TO AVOID THE BLAME GAME

- "It might be a good idea if . . ."
- "When you_____, I feel _____."
- "When I have trouble with _____, I always_____."
- "I'm good at organizing things; maybe I could give you hand with that."
- "I've noticed we've both been really busy lately. I think we should talk about how to handle house stuff when we have crazy weeks."

COMPROMISE: YOUR OWN ROOMMATE PEACE TREATY

It's in everybody's best interests to compromise. Sometimes it happens in small ways, and you don't even know you're doing it. Like the way I would always take the trash out and Sophie would always deal with the recycling. We never designated those jobs; they were just things we automatically did, and each of us appreciated it. I don't know why, but I'm terrible at remembering the recycling. But it doesn't bother me one bit to heave that nasty trash into the Dumpster whenever the bag is full.

Most of the time, however, compromises are things that need to be openly agreed on, as well as reasonable and realistic. It makes no sense to come up with a compromise that only one or none of your roommates can live with. The key is to find common ground whenever a problem crops up, and then arrive at an accommodation that everyone can live with.

For example, another roommate of mine, Christina, wanted me to stop leaving my clothing on the couch. I knew that in my daily rush to

MULTIPLE ROOMMATES

W hen you have five or six people living together in a house or large apartment, the possibility of conflicts and misunderstanding increases exponentially. I've seen large groups of roommates work this out a couple of different ways. Either

1. The roommates are such good friends that they put their friendships ahead of the small stuff—everyone takes care of the dirty dishes and household messes in a laissez-faire, "I'll scratch your back, you scratch mine (later)" sort of way

or

2. They have developed house rules to deal with the mess—rules that for sanity's sake should be followed.

---

get dressed, this simply wasn't going to happen—old habits die hard, and my closet was practically in the living room. So we talked it over and agreed that I would make sure that once the hectic part of my day was done, I'd put my clothes back into the closet or at least throw them into my room and out of the way. See? Compromise.

Here's another scenario: You and your roommate have different pay schedules at work. You like to pay the bills right away, but because her check comes only once a month, she isn't always able to pay right away. So maybe you agree that you'll cover her part of the bill until her check comes, or you'll pay the bill a week later, rather than right away. *Compromise.* As long as you do, you'll have an excellent chance of making your living experience together—and your relationship— work.

— FIVE WAYS TO KEEP A COOL HEAD — WHEN HOUSEHOLD PROBLEMS HEAT UP

Y our roommate has left dirty clothes all over the apartment or forgotten to pay the electric bill or woken you up by blasting the stereo after midnight—*again*. Naturally, you're upset—but before you let fly with a few choice words, consider these tips:

- **GIVE PROBLEMS A DAY OR TWO TO SETTLE.** When something really bothers us, it's often because a lot of other things are bothering us as well. Before you sit your roommate down for a big discussion, let the issue settle for a couple of days. By then you may find it's not even worth bringing the problem up—and if you do, you'll be ready to talk it over calmly and constructively.

- **DON'T LET THINGS FESTER.** While it's a good idea to wait a day or two, don't wait any longer than that to discuss the problem, or your roommate may feel like you're holding a grudge. Waiting too long can also cause resentments to build so that by the time you do discuss the problem you're ready to blow.

- **APPROACH THE PROBLEM WITH AN OPEN MIND.** If you go into a house meeting or roommate discussion with the idea that everything will go your way, you may soon find yourself in the middle of a shouting match. Instead, go in with an open mind. Just as you have your reasons for feeling upset, your roommate might have legitimate reasons for handling things the way he or she did.

- **THINK ABOUT OPTIONS.** Before you talk things over with your roommate, come up with two or three possible solutions to the problem and be ready to present them. Of course you'll still want to wait and hear what your roommate has to say—but

CONTINUED ➡

having some ideas ready will show your roommate that you're thinking actively about how to make things better for everyone.

• **PICK A GOOD TIME TO TALK.** Choose a time when everyone is relaxed and comfortable. If your roommate has just gotten home from a long day at work or a tough class or has just come off a traumatic phone call, it's probably *not* a good time to discuss household issues. If your roommate seems to have a lot of bad days, schedule a time a day or two from now when you can sit down and talk together about the problem. That way, it won't seem like you're springing it on her out of the blue.

COMMITMENT: WHERE YOU MAKE IT OR BREAK IT

Now that you and your roomie have discussed the issues, come to a compromise, and agreed to make it work, all that's left is to stick to your part of the bargain. You'd think this would be the easy part, but it's not always so simple. Like a New Year's resolution, the plan will work only if you commit to *making* it work. It might take a week or two for your responsibilities to become second nature, but once they do, your home life will purr like a well-oiled machine. Just be sure to check in with each other from time to time to ensure that the commitment is still being met.

If everybody commits to the compromise, smooth sailin', baby! Welcome to your happy home.

And if that's not the case? If your bathroom still isn't getting cleaned on a regular basis and the garbage is being taken out only when it begins to overflow the can, then it's time to start communicating again. Obviously, Plan A didn't work, so you'll need to formulate a Plan B.

Sometimes it helps to draw up a schedule of who will do what first, in order to get the commitment aspect of your peace treaty going. You can even go so far as to set up consequences for when someone isn't living up to expectations. You may think this sounds controlling (I can practically hear you saying, "Okay, Mom"), but it actually works. Here's a great example: In my friend's apartment, if you don't do your dishes in a timely manner, they get dumped in your room for you to deal with. In that household, you'd better believe dishes get done in a timely manner.

Remember, the issue is not whether the living room should be vacuumed every week, or whether the dishes should be done right away or left until every dish is dirty or who scrubs the bathroom. What's important is that you and your roommate are all comfortable with the levels of effort being exerted in taking care of the space you share together.

CHAPTER 2

YOUR NEW PLACE

WHETHER THIS IS your first time living away from home or you've moved seven times before, every new place brings with it new expectations, relationships, and lifestyles that you'll need to handle. Two of these relationships are especially important, because they affect virtually every aspect of your daily life. The first is your relationship with your roommates; the second is your relationship with your landlord.

In the next chapter, we'll deal with the nitty-gritty of how to get along with your roommates on a daily basis. But the first—and most important—step toward having a happy home is picking the right people to live with.

CHOOSING YOUR ROOMMATES

The first thing you need to do is to decide how many people you want to live with. Aha! This is a difficult question if you've never lived with

WHEN YOU'RE NEW IN TOWN

Nothing is harder than being a newcomer in a place where you don't know anyone. Even if you can afford to live on your own, roommates can be a great help in making new friends in a strange town. To find ads for roommates wanted or available rooms, check your local paper as well as online message boards like Craigslist. You can also post your own ad for a roommate or sign up with a roommate-matching service.

roommates before. Here are some points to consider when determining how many other people you can comfortably coexist with:

- Every additional roommate brings their own set of friends with them. If you share a house with four other people, that means five groups of friends will be cycling through your home. Is this something you're prepared to handle?

- The more roommates there are, the more complicated it becomes to manage household responsibilities.

- Do you crave privacy or need absolute quiet to concentrate? If so, you may do best with one or two roommates—or even a place of your own, if you can afford it.

Once you've decided how many people you can comfortably live with, it's time to search for roommates. Many people start off by considering their friends. But before you start talking to your pal about moving in together, it's worth spending a little time thinking about what qualities you're looking for in a roommate. If your friend fits the bill, great; if not, seriously consider looking elsewhere. You'll save yourself a lot of stress down the road, and maybe even your friendship.

Here's a checklist to get you started:

PROSPECTIVE ROOMMATE CHECKLIST

FINANCIAL
— What kind of a budget is this person on?
— Can this person be relied on to share the monthly bills for basic expenditures such as rent, electric, water, phone, and heating/air-conditioning?
— Is this person interested in contributing for extras like cable or Internet fees?

LIFE SCHEDULE
— Is this person a student?
— Is this person a night worker or a day worker?
— Is this person away for most of the day or at home all the time?
— Is this person a party animal or antisocial?
— Does this person have houseguests often? (This can be a big issue for some people.)

PERSONAL LIFE CHOICES
— Drinking/drugs
— Sex life
— Vegan/vegetarian/omnivore
— Religious beliefs
— Smoking

HOUSEHOLD RESPONSIBILITIES
— What kind of a dishwashing philosophy does this person have? (Wash right after using, or let the dishes sit till there's a large stack to wash?)
— Is this person willing to pitch in on vacuuming, mopping, and clearing away clutter?

SLEEPING HABITS

___ Is this person sensitive to sound when he or she is sleeping? (I've seen this become a serious issue, especially in a place with thin walls.)

___ Is this person asleep during the day and awake at night?

SIGNIFICANT OTHERS

___ Does your potential roommate have a significant other?

___ Does the significant other have his or her own place?

___ How often is the significant other likely to be staying overnight at your place?

PERSONAL PREFERENCES

___ TV: Does this person watch a lot, a little, or none? Do they mind that you watch a lot, a little, or none?

___ Music. What type of music does this person like and how loud, and when do they like to listen to it?

___ Does this person prefer to go out or stay in? (A roommate who stays in more may have their friends over a lot. Someone who goes out a lot might be difficult to get ahold of.)

You must, must, *must* be honest about your lifestyle and habits when talking to potential roommates—and vice versa. It would be very unfair if you signed a lease only to find out later that your roommate uses recreational drugs that you're uncomfortable with or refuses to discuss how the household responsibilities should be managed or has a habit of falling asleep in the living room instead of in her bed.

THE GOOD, THE BAD, THE LANDLORD

I was psyched: My current lease was almost up, and my roommate and I had just seen a decent place that had everything we needed. We put our names on the lease hours later. Signed, sealed, delivered. We had a new place to live.

In our haste, we didn't even think of checking out what kind of a landlord we had acquired. All we knew was that he had just bought the apartment, and we had just signed a one-year lease. As it turned out, we were in for a year of ignored phone calls, unfinished projects, electrical fiascos—and did I mention a lot of stress? Had we known that this particular landlord had a reputation for not showing up, I'm not sure we would have ever signed that lease.

Unfortunately, when it comes to landlords, you're going to encounter the good, the bad, and the ugly. I accepted the fact that the kitchen in my old apartment couldn't handle a microwave because the outlets didn't carry enough wattage. After four months of living without a microwave,

HEADS UP: TAKE PICTURES BEFORE MOVING IN

It's always a good idea to snap some photos of your new place *before* you unpack and move in. Cracks in the wall, scrapes on the floor, and carpet stains, no matter how minor they may seem, are all things you'll want to document and date, so you won't run the risk of being accused of causing the damage yourself (and having to pay for the repairs).

however, I learned that the city I lived in required every kitchen of every home to have such an outlet. I let my landlord know that he wasn't up to code, and eventually the problem was fixed.

This example demonstrates why your single most important safeguard as a tenant is to know your rights. This is easier than you may think: all you have to do is call your city's information department or town clerk and ask where you can find the laws regarding landlord and tenant rights. The local housing authority or department can usually help you as well.

THE CONSIDERATE TENANT

Hopefully, your landlord will be a lot more responsive than mine was, and you'll quickly settle into a friendly, mutually respectful relationship. You can help this process along by being a thoughtful, responsible tenant. Here are a few tips for getting on your landlord's good side.

- *Pay your rent on time.* Being prompt with your rent payments—having your check in his mailbox on the first of the month, if that's what the lease calls for—shows your landlord not only that you're living up to your agreement but that you take this responsibility seriously.

- *Respond to your landlord's calls right away.* This is a good thing to remember when dealing with anyone—but when it comes to your landlord, you want to return any calls as promptly as possible. It will help get the job done more quickly, plus your landlord can't then justify his delays with the excuse that you've been difficult to reach.

- *Be on time for meetings.* Anytime you're scheduled to meet with your landlord, either to let him into your apartment or to discuss repairs, it's essential to be on time. If you're on time, things will get done, and he has nothing to complain about. If you're running late and don't let him know, on the other hand, you risk a cancelled meeting and a ticked-off landlord.

• ***Clean up before your landlord drops by.*** If your landlord comes over and your apartment is a disaster, she's not going to see you in the best of lights. Straightening up before she or any maintenance workers arrive does two things: First, it shows that you are responsible about caring for your living space, and second, it's simply a considerate thing to do. I wouldn't want to be Mr. Fix-It and have to climb over some tenant's dirty underwear or work around a pile of week-old dirty dishes.

• ***Don't try to beat the system.*** If your lease forbids you from smoking in the house or having pets and you do so anyway, you're in violation of your lease—and if your landlord catches you, he has the right to evict you. So play it safe, either by finding a place where you can live the way you'd like to or by complying honestly with the rules of your lease.

WHEN YOUR LANDLORD DOESN'T PLAY FAIR

It may be that you're well informed about your rights and doing everything a model tenant should, but you find yourself dealing with a slumlord who simply doesn't care. For those of you who've never experienced it, a slumlord can be an infuriating presence (or absence) in your life: Things don't get fixed when they should, money keeps getting sucked out of you, and you end up wasting a considerable amount of time chasing after him in hopes of getting even the most basic problems attended to.

DON'T MAKE MY MISTAKE

I tried withholding rent from a landlord once and failed to write to him or open an escrow account, which holds the money but doesn't allow the landlord to touch it until he's fixed what needs fixing. He wound up charging me for two weeks' worth of late rent—and I couldn't do anything about it.

If your landlord isn't playing fair, it's easy to think that withholding your rent or taking your landlord to court is necessary—but it might not be. Here are the steps to take when your landlord isn't holding up his end of the lease:

First: Document Everything

I can't stress this enough! Any time you ask your landlord to fix something or reimburse you for a repair, you should *document your request in writing*. If you feel you need to file a formal complaint or withhold your rent, be sure you know what your legal rights are before taking action. Should you get to the point where you need to withhold your rent, you will have to write the landlord a letter of notification. Photocopy this letter for your own records. In fact, keep a copy of *all* your correspondence with the landlord, as well as a phone log of any conversations you have, and note all times and dates. These written records will be critical if your situation ever reaches the legal intervention stage.

Second: Be Nice—It Gets the Job Done Faster

When discussing a needed repair or other issue with your landlord, be as friendly and as understanding as you can. No one is going to be eager to help out a young person who whines and moans. State clearly and completely what the problem is and ask when he might be able to handle it. Set a date and time for your landlord to come and take a look at the problem. Be prepared to show some patience and flexibility; some landlords have full-time jobs on top of running their properties, and often can't be Mr. Fix-It-Right-Away. By the same token, however, your landlord is contractually obligated to fix the problems in your living space. When you do set a date, be gracious and appreciative, and thank your landlord for taking the time to come and look at the problem.

Third: The City Runs on Real-World Time

After your landlord comes by to assess your problem, he may need to call in someone else to fix it. Unfortunately, the real world moves in real-world time. Be as patient and understanding as you can be with your landlord and any Mr. Fix-It who comes to your apartment, for they may be called upon to do more for you in the future. Recognize that they're here to help you and make your life easier.

If your landlord continues to stonewall and you have to get the city involved, you'll need to be even more patient. Remember that your

HOLDING UP YOUR END OF THE BARGAIN

When you hold up your end of the rental agreement—by paying your rent on time, complying with the rules your landlord has set for the apartment (smoking, pets, etc.), and staying in good favor with your neighbors—you deprive your landlord of any reason not to hold up *his* end of the bargain. It's also important to treat your landlord with respect, even if you don't think he deserves it. Acting like a jerk, either over the phone or in person, will only make him less willing to help you—and more apt to give you less than stellar service.

landlord has to abide by what city officials decide—and these decisions can take time. Cities deal with slumlords all the time, some of whom are very good at avoiding compliance with the rules. So bide your time and let the wheels of government turn, knowing that you're taking the right steps.

Fourth: Save Yourself Some Stress—Let It Go

Finally, a very hard lesson I've had to learn myself is that it's sometimes best to just let the issue go. If the problem in your apartment or house is serious or presents a safety concern, it's important to get it taken care of. But if it's something simple and your landlord is being completely unhelpful, you may just have to take a deep breath and tell yourself, *the lease is up in 3 months*—and let it go. When I first moved into one apartment, the ceiling in the bathroom was collecting water, which then leaked down the shelves. My landlord did show up to repair the leak, but he left a large hole in the ceiling and never fixed it. It sure wasn't pretty to look at, but it wasn't causing any harm. I let it go.

CHAPTER 3

TOP FIVE POTENTIAL WAR ZONES AT HOME

T HE LEASE IS SIGNED. Moving day has come and gone. You're doing it: living in your own place with people you chose to live with. You've got your room all set up, everything is stored in the bathroom and kitchen, and your living room is *way* cooler than your other friends'. Now you can kick back and enjoy, right?

Ah, but be careful: Amid the friends coming over, the downtime to yourself, and the utter elation you feel walking into your very own place, every home has land mines just waiting to blow. We tiptoe around them: the dirty socks, the disheveled living room, the dishes, the food, the globs of toothpaste stuck in the sink like stalagmites, the late-night noise, the borrowed shirt that's now ruined! It all becomes too much, until you just . . . can't . . . take it . . . anymore. Then, *Boom!*—there you are, standing in the living room, fists clenched, breathing heavily, eyes shifting from roommate to roommate as they look at you watchfully, trying not to make any sudden movements. *Ohh-kaay,* you sense each of them thinking, *she's finally cracked.*

The potential for problems to arise in your home is stealthier than you might think. In particular, there are five potential war zones that you'll need to watch out for:

- The kitchen

- The bathroom

- The living room

- Noise

- Other people's stuff

The kitchen, the bathroom, and the living room make up the common spaces in your home. And in any common space (especially if you live with several other people) things can get a bit messy. This can result in one of two problems: Either you're making the mess and leaving it for your roommates to clean up or you find that you're constantly cleaning up both your mess and theirs—in which case I say, *stop!*—you're not a maid.

Tensions can also mount when you create noise at a time when your roommates need quiet, or vice versa. Borrowing other people's stuff is another action that can really touch a nerve. You and your roommate may start out with one happy, communal closet; but the first time an item goes missing or gets ruined, the closets separate and distrust settles in.

This may sound a bit grim, I know, but don't worry. The whole idea here is to identify potential problems *before* they can turn into crises. Once you do, you can then use your skills of communication, compromise, and commitment to work out a solution for living harmoniously and happily together.

THE KITCHEN

Messy kitchens are one of the most common sources of roommate conflict. What mostly goes on in the kitchen? *Cooking and eating.* And what aspects of these activities have the most potential to cause problems? *Dishes and food.*

Let's begin with the kitchen sink.

Dish Wars: Coming Soon to an Apartment Near You

I remember arriving home one wintry evening from a weekend out of town, lugging bags of groceries and all set to cook a great dinner. When I stepped into the kitchen I could see immediately that it was a disaster. Even if I'd wanted to deal with the mess, there was simply no room to clean. Plus, with everything dirty, I had nothing to cook with, and no clean dishes to eat from. It was clear that my roommate had had a busy weekend, but *hello!*—it was now Tuesday night, around 8:30, and I was starving and feeling no obligation whatsoever to clean up the kitchen.

I walked straight to Christina's room and poked my head in.

"Hi . . . I know you have to study right now for your exam, but there are no clean pans to cook with or utensils to eat with. Do you think you could please come do a few dishes so that I can make dinner?"

And then it happened: the look, the narrowed eyes, the stony expression, the pause, and finally the cold but compliant response: "Fine."

Christina and I butted heads that evening in a big way. Fortunately our dish war ended almost as soon as it began. At around 1 AM, we found ourselves in the living room, both feeling guilty. We quickly came to an agreement that we'd each do our own dishes, except for those instances when one of us was swamped with work, in which case the other person would do her a favor and help out.

This issue may seem trivial, but it's not. Dishes in the kitchen can be an extremely sore subject between roommates. In your newly independent life, you may find yourself living without the automatic dishwasher you grew up with. Each person also has his or her own philosophy and strategies for tackling a dish-infested sink. In addition, a person's willingness to tackle dishwashing is often based on mood, or how busy he or she is with other pressing matters like work or school.

Communication is the first step to solving the problem. If you and your roommates *talk* about your kitchen preferences, you'll understand where the others are coming from. (See "Choosing Your Roommates," page 13.) Some people want a clean kitchen all the time. Others can stand a mess for a day or two. Still others will leave a mess until all the dishes are dirty and the only solution is to clean up or eat out. The best way to avoid a dish war is to communicate about the problem, agree on a compromise, and commit to the solution.

For example, Kate, who's a clean freak, and Maggie, who just doesn't care, live together. After a few initial skirmishes, they agreed to establish a two-day minimum for how long dishes can be left in the sink. Kate might wash her pots and pans right after she sits down to eat, while Maggie lets her pots, pans, and dishes sit till the following day—but eventually the dishes all get done.

DIRTY DISHES: A COLORFUL SOLUTION

I know five girls who all live in the same house but who rarely have a dispute about whose dishes are in the sink. The reason: To avoid kitchen conflicts, each person bought an inexpensive set of plates, bowls, and silverware in a specific color. Each person simply uses and cleans her own set.

INSTANT TIP

W hen you and your roommate cook meals together, try cleaning up as you go. One roommate cooks while the other cleans the pots and pans used in cooking. Then you both help out with the rest of the dishes after you've eaten. It's so simple!

If someone isn't living up to their end of the agreement, that needs to be addressed, too. My friend Estelle got so sick of playing the maid to her roommates that she ended up taking their dirty dishes and putting them right inside the front door. When her roommates came home, the dishes were the first thing they saw. They got the message.

Food or Foe?

Starving, you trudge home at 8 PM after the three-hour class that tops off your busy day. Visions of the wonderful leftover stir-fry sitting in the fridge fill your mind. You can almost taste the teriyaki. Walking into the house, you dive into the fridge, searching for the Tupperware container that holds last night's dinner. It's nowhere in sight.

"Dude, did you eat the stir-fry we made last night?" you ask your roommate who's been home since 4 PM.

"Yeah, I heated it up when I got home," comes the cheerful, full-bellied reply. "Why?"

"*Why?!*" you shout. "Because I've been dreaming of it all afternoon, *that's* why! Just *once* I'd like to get a chance to eat the leftovers! I mean, you had time to cook! I've been in class all day! Now I have to cook, *and* there are no clean dishes!"

After this incident, my roommate and I decided to leave little notes on our dry-erase board along the lines of "Please don't touch the leftovers." Sometimes we'd even discuss it as we were cleaning up from dinner and putting the leftovers away.

When you're living with roommates, finishing someone else's leftovers without asking is a huge issue. The loss of a chicken leg or a piece of pie has a way of turning normal people into food-hoarding mongrels. The only solution is to set firm house standards about eating food that isn't yours. My personal take on it is: If the food is mine—that is, something I purchased or cooked without you—then I'd appreciate it if you would ask before helping yourself. And please—*don't* finish my leftovers. I bought the food, I cooked the meal, and I'd like to eat it.

I've been very lucky to live with only one other person at a time. Many of my friends who've lived in four- or five-person houses have had numerous run-ins over the filching of food. For instance, the roommates might all decide they'll each shop separately; then, the next thing you know, Reese is scarfing up spoonfuls of Matt's peanut butter when Matt isn't around. Bottom line: Take responsibility for yourself and buy your own peanut butter! Know which food is yours, and which is your roommates'—then keep your hands off their food, unless it's offered to you. If everyone sticks to the ground rules of the kitchen, there will be no disputes over who ate what.

Shopping for Groceries

Here are three things to consider before you and your roommates head to the grocery store:

1. What kind of food do you eat?

There's no sense in combining your grocery shopping with your roommates' if you like to eat totally different things, or if one of you eats out all the time and the others always cook in. Even if you have divergent tastes, however, you should consider shopping together and sharing expenses for such kitchen staples as spices, condiments, and paper towels as well as any other foods or kitchen supplies that you all use on a regular basis.

2. How much do you eat?

I'm not a math major, but I do know that if you eat two eggs for breakfast and your roommate eats four, you're going to end up feeling you're getting the raw end of the deal. Make a point of discussing how to share costs fairly and proportionately—then review this arrangement every few months.

3. How much money do you have to spend?

If you're still in school and can only afford $50 a week on groceries while your roommate is pulling down a good salary, obviously your roommate will be able to spend more on food than you will. That's why it's important to sit down with your roommate(s) and discuss food budgeting. You may determine that the best approach is every person for themselves; or, if you're both on a tight budget, you can explore ways to stretch your dollar by shopping and cooking together.

Shopping together all of the time works well if you have similar eating styles and budgets. My roommate Christina and I found this worked best for us. We would always buy staples together (chicken, eggs, veggies, milk, etc.), and then we'd each choose a few extra items that one of us might not care for but the other enjoyed (coffee, oranges, cookies). We didn't worry about paying for these items separately; we just figured they'd equal out in the end.

If you have totally different eating styles and budgets, on the other hand, you may find there's no real point in shopping together. Caroline and her former roommate used to shop jointly, until they realized that they were eating very different foods in different amounts. So they decided to shop and store their food separately. Each got a shelf in the fridge and a cupboard in the kitchen. Leftovers belonged to the person who cooked the meal. Caroline and her roommate didn't get upset

HEADS UP: CLEANING SUPPLIES

You and your roommates have come to agreements about bills, rent, and food. But what about cleaning supplies and other household items—things that are certainly part of the budget but that you won't need to buy every time you go to the grocery store? Discuss with your roommates what type of cleaning supplies you need, and how much you'll each pitch in for them. Here are some items worth including in this discussion:

- Dish soap
- Sponges
- Vacuum cleaner bags
- Paper towels
- All-purpose cleaning agent

- Toilet paper
- Laundry detergent
- Damp mop or mop
- Glass cleaner
- Bath soap

over leftovers occasionally being eaten by the noncook or the borrowing of milk, because they'd laid down the ground rules: Nothing was ever borrowed in excess or finished without being replaced. They both found that this relaxed but respectful attitude toward food made living together a real pleasure.

THE BATHROOM

It's a very private space, which everyone uses.

The bathroom is where we take care of our personal hygiene. It's a space we're not eager to share with people we know, let alone people we don't know. In a perfect world, we would each have our own bathroom and no one else would use it.

Unfortunately, it's not a perfect world. In all likelihood you do share a bathroom, not only with roommates but also with friends of roommates. So until everyone is granted his or her own personal facility by universal decree, you'll have to do your best to avoid potential conflicts over bathroom issues.

Because the bathroom is a place that everyone uses, including guests, special care should be taken to leave it in reasonably good condition for the next person to use, whether they are going to be showering or

A SITUATION THAT WENT DOWN THE DRAIN

Christina moved into a new apartment with three guys and another girl. The apartment had two bathrooms, so they decided to designate one as a "girl's" bathroom and the other a "guy's" bathroom. Christina and her roommate Danielle were pleased, because they felt they'd gotten the good end of the deal. They fixed up their bathroom and kept it clean, and for a while everything was fine.

Things didn't go according to plan, however: The guys never got around to installing a shower curtain, so they ended up using the girls' shower. Then one of the guys had three guests for the weekend, and they all used the girls' shower as well. So now *eight* people were using Christina and Danielle's shower.

Eventually, the drain draineth no more. To make matters worse, the host of the three guests refused to take any responsibility for the now nonworking shower.

Out of this disaster came a new house rule: Any roommate who has a guest was responsible for any mess or problem that the guest did not take care of.

Lesson one: Set some ground rules for guests.

Lesson two: If you have more than one bathroom, encourage everyone in the house to get all bathrooms set up as soon as possible, so that everyone is using the space they agreed upon.

BATHROOM CLEANING CHECKLIST

Wipe down: sink, shower, toilet, mirror, doorknob

Clear away: shaving supplies, makeup, hair products, toothbrush, toothpaste, and dental floss

Restock: toilet paper, soap, hand towels

Mop: floor

Empty: the trash

---

simply looking in the mirror. In a two-gender household, that also means always putting the seat down on the toilet after using it.

You and your housemates should take the time to discuss bathroom standards: In what shape would you like your bathroom to be left after use? Does it matter if there are little pools of water on the counter, or should you wipe them up every time you use the sink? What about removing hair from the drain? My hair is quite long, so if I don't clean the drain on a regular basis, it's Drano Central for me. What about that empty roll of toilet paper that never made it to the garbage, so that the new roll now sits on the wet sink? Where do the shaving supplies, deodorant, makeup, hair products, and nail polish get stored?

Your bathroom doesn't necessarily have to be sparkling clean all the time, but when it is a shared space, it needs to be at a level of cleanliness that everyone feels comfortable with. If everyone agrees on a standard and sticks to it, you should have no problem sharing a bathroom.

THE LIVING ROOM

The living room may look harmless, but it's full of hidden dangers. Here are a few to be especially aware of.

The Trail

A great *Calvin and Hobbs* cartoon by Bill Waterson shows Calvin's mom picking up a sweater, then some shoes, then a wet jacket left on the floor by the open front door. Calvin saunters past, saying, "I'm home," to which his mom gives a "go figure" look and says, "So I gathered."

Every time I entered my old apartment, a trail of shoes, bag, books, keys, wallet, cell phone, and sweater seemed to practically shed off of me. And when I dressed to go out, even in the morning, a trail documenting the outfits I'd rejected would spread across the floor. Having a clothing closet in the hallway didn't help.

Finally, my roommate Christina told me she felt as if my life was splattered all over the place. She said this on a day when the apartment was messy—and, as we looked around, I saw that the mess was all mine. She added that even if she wanted to clean while I was in class, it would be pointless because my stuff was everywhere and she didn't feel it was her responsibility to clean it up in the first place. And she was right—it

INSTANT TIP

Try designating specific areas for things such as shoes, jackets, keys, and sunglasses. That way, if you find yourself shedding your stuff when you walk in the door, at least you'll have agreed-upon places to put things.

wasn't. So, we started compromising. First, Christina said that if she ever did a surprise housecleaning, she would simply dump my clothing on the floor in my room. I countered by offering to wake up ten minutes earlier so I'd have time to dump *my own* rejected outfits in my room. I knew I wasn't going to be able to stop myself from trying something on, not liking it, and dropping it on the floor—so the extra ten minutes gave me time to clean up after I was comfortably dressed.

Getting in the spirit of things, we also bought a coat stand and designated an area for shoes and boots. These improvements made a big difference in helping me keep my life from trailing behind me.

The Living Room as Dining Room

If your kitchen is too small for any kind of a table and there's no dining area, the living-room couch and coffee table become the place to eat, watch TV, and entertain, all in one. When you live in this type of situation, it's especially easy for dishes to be left in the living room and food crumbs to adorn the furniture and floor. The living room/dining room is definitely a place where you and your roommates want to agree on some ground rules.

For instance, maybe you decide not to put a rug in the living room, so that it's easier to clean up crumbs and spills. Or, if you have a kitchen table, you might decide that no food is allowed in the living room.

The Battle of the Clicker

This is an issue that seems to plague families, friends, roommates, and couples alike. It's a real shame that such difficulties arise from such a useful device. When custody of the clicker is the issue, there are a couple of ways to sort out the problem: If you opted not to sign up for cable but your roommates did, that pretty much takes you out of the running for channel control. If you're all chipping in on the cable bill, then the best solution is to *communicate* about what you want to watch. Unless you get another television, you're all going to have to share screen time. Has one roommate really taken over the TV? Then it may be time to have a house meeting and put your "three C's" into practice. With a little scheduling and the creative use of digital recording (see "TV Alternatives," page 36), you should able to convince your clicker-monopolizing roommate to yield control.

When Jill and another girl lived with three guys who were avid sports fans, the girls found they never got to watch TV. No matter what day or time it was, there always seemed to be a game on. As a final resort, the girls took the *TV Guide* and highlighted all the games the guys watched. Then they sat the guys down and literally pointed out how much television time they were eating up watching sports.

The guys did agree—however begrudgingly—that they could listen to many of the games on the radio. They also made a counter-request: that when a "big" game was on, they could watch it on the tube. The result: The girls got to watch their shows, the guys got to see their major games, and no one had to miss out. The girls also understood that reruns of shows will happen—while reruns of games won't.

Finally, here are two other etiquette tips to keep in mind when watching the tube:

- **First come, first served.** If someone is already watching, it's generally a bad idea to walk in and change the channel. A little consideration goes a long way here. Since the TV in the living room is a shared device, the best-case scenario is if everyone agrees to watch the same thing. Otherwise, it's first come, first served.

- **Don't hog the remote.** If you have custody of the clicker, find a channel you like and then put the remote on the coffee table. Personally, I've never freaked out over people hogging the remote, but a lot of people can't stand it when another person starts

— TV ALTERNATIVES

I f television time has become a bit of a sore spot in your house or apartment, here's a really simple solution: Go watch your favorite show at a friend's place, or take in the Patriots versus the Giants at a bar. Just because the TV at home is currently unavailable, it doesn't mean that you can't enjoy your program somewhere else.

Another good idea, especially if you live with more than two or three people, is to get TiVo or a similar digital recording device that lets you record one show while watching another. Besides being incredibly convenient, it's really not that expensive when you split the cost—and it makes a world of difference between roommates. Many cable providers now offer some version of this service, making it easily accessible if you already have cable or satellite.

---

channel surfing during commercials, messes with the volume, or flips through the interactive guide at the bottom of the screen while the show is going on. (My dad's friend disliked having his kids hog the remotes so much that he tied them to his easy chair.) It's okay to flip channels as long as nobody else minds. But hogging the remote is something we need to let go of.

NOISE

Noise is a two-way street: We all want to able to make noise at times, and we all crave quiet at some point. Whether you tend to make noise at 2 AM and want quiet at noon or vice-versa, you and your roommates need to come to an understanding about what noise is acceptable and when. If you're unable to work or study outside your home, for example,

I LIKE IT QUIET NOW, BUT I LIKE TO MAKE NOISE WHEN ...

D on't you hate it? Whenever you want it quiet, it seems there's always a great reason to party, and whenever you're ready to party, there's an important reason to keep your place quiet. How your noise affects your roommates, and vice versa, really depends on everyone's schedules and noise tolerance. There are times when having friends over—or even making a phone call—can be too much noise.

Things That Make Noise	Things To Be Quiet For
• Parties	• Work
• Moving	• Study
• Telephone calls	• Sleep
• Music	• Movies
• TV	• Decompressing
• Coming home late	

determining how you can work and your housemates can play simultaneously will be important. This may mean designating a workroom away from much of the noise. Or, if you don't have the space for a workroom, agree on times when you'll both need the house to be quiet.

Make a point of discussing your "noise schedules" with each other, including any special needs you may have. (See box above.) Whenever you get back from a long trip, for instance, maybe you really need to be alone to decompress. By your mentioning this to your roommate, he or she will understand that these are good times to take a walk, run errands, or meet up with friends.

OTHER PEOPLE'S STUFF

If you're looking for one simple rule about borrowing, here it is: If you can't guarantee that the item will be returned exactly as it was when you received it, don't borrow it.

For those of you who want to know about the gray areas, please read on.

Borrowing from friends, roommates, family, or significant others carries certain responsibilities. Essentially, when you borrow or use someone's things, you are taking responsibility for them. I was really appreciative when Christina told me that she had gotten charcoal on my rug in the living room and had taken steps to clean it up. She took responsibility for the mishap and apologized. Accidents do happen, but that doesn't change the fact that *if you borrow or use something, you are responsible for it.*

When it comes to borrowing clothing, my roommates and I have all done a good job of setting limits. We decide what can and can't be borrowed, what can be borrowed without asking, and what must be asked for. We respect these limits, and know how to care for whatever it is we borrow: Certain shirts must be hung up; others can be folded

INSTANT TIP

Never borrow something if you think a roommate would be upset by it. Certain things are just off limits. For example, when Christina and I lived together, for the most part our closets were open to each other. I didn't know that a certain button-down shirt was particularly special to her, and borrowed it one day. Luckily, Chris was good about it: She calmly let me know that she preferred I not wear it again, and I didn't. Even though the shirt looked plain to me, it clearly held great sentimental value to her.

NOT SO SEXY THE NEXT DAY

ngela has trouble with her roommate Gabby borrowing her clothing. For one thing, Gabby is completely supported by her parents, whereas Angela is financially independent. For Angela, this makes things like clothing, jewelry, and shoes just a little harder to come by. One day, Gabby let herself into Angela's room, rummaged through her closet, and found a great shirt to wear. Gabby went out and had a great time in Angela's shirt; she danced all night, had quite a few drinks, then headed home with her boyfriend. She felt confident in the shirt all night long—maybe a little too confident.

The next day, when Angela had learned that her shirt had been borrowed without permission, she asked what had happened to it. Giggling, Gabby said, "You won't believe it. Last night, Jon and I got home and he threw me onto the bed and we started making out, and he ripped the shirt right off of me! Isn't that so animal-like and sexy?"

"No, actually, it's not," Angela, said, quietly fuming. "It wasn't your shirt he ripped, it was mine."

Gabby was never allowed to wear Angela's clothes again. And Angela had a lock put on her bedroom door.

---

back in the drawer. Some items I prefer to wash myself, other things I'd rather the borrower wash, and sometimes I don't even care if it's been washed before it's returned. The point is, the rules for borrowing clothing have been established *before* the borrowing takes place.

It's also a good idea to keep track of anything you lend out. My friend Margot has a "borrowing book." Whether the loan is clothing, books, or money, she writes down everything: who borrows the item, what item is borrowed, and when it will be returned. Maybe this strikes you as overkill, but after a friend borrowed Margot's favorite dress and $50 to pay bills—neither of which Margot saw again—she

THE FOUR CARDINAL RULES OF BORROWING

1. Discuss what is off-limits or freely usable.

2. Don't borrow without asking.

3. You are responsible for what you borrow.

4. Don't lend out items you really care about.

decided to keep track of who got what and when. "I don't mind lending stuff out," she says. "I just want to make sure I get it back."

The Big Borrow

The car. It's so easy to just say, "Sure, the keys are on the table; go ahead." However, before you, the borrower, walk out whistling, stop and think: Borrowing someone else's car—or loaning your car out to someone else—carries with it a lot of responsibility.

If you're thinking of borrowing a car, before you take the keys, ask yourself:

- Do I have the money to replace the car?

- If I get pulled over, even for something like a burned-out taillight, do I have insurance, a license, and registration to show the officer?

- Is the car's maintenance up-to-date? What if I get pulled over and the car is five months overdue for inspection?

If you're thinking of loaning your car, ask yourself:

- Is this person's license in good standing, and do I know what my liability is as the registered driver of the vehicle if it isn't?

- What if someone is injured? Do I know what my coverage is, and how it is affected by letting somone else drive my vehicle?

Creating a home environment that is comfortable and cooperative is a big step in the process of gaining true independence. It will also make your place much more inviting for those who come to visit. By applying the principles of consideration, respect, and honesty to the five potential war zones of your house, and then employing the strategies of communication, compromise, and commitment, you and your roommates should be able to sidestep any land mines, hidden or otherwise. And that way, no one goes *boom*.

CHAPTER 4

HELLO, NEIGHBOR

WHEN I FIRST MOVED in to my apartment, I used to refer to the man who lived next door as "the guy who parks his expensive car so that it takes up two spaces." Then one day, after I'd been living there a few months, I actually took the time to see *him* and not his parking job.

He's about my parents' age. . . . He mows his lawn on the weekend . . . waxes the car. . . . Wife must take care of the flowers. . . . Oh no! He saw me watching him. Wait—he's waving. (I waved back a little timidly.) *Uh-oh, he's coming over here!*

"Hey, how are you doing? You just move in here?" He wore a big smile.

I extended my hand. "Yes, in June."

"Nice to meet you. I'm Keith Greenford," he said. "You a student up at UVM?"

"Yup, I'm going to be a junior this fall."

"Tough year. What's your major?"

Mr. Greenford and I talked for about half an hour. He's lived on my street for more than twenty-five years, and he told me the whole history of how my landlord wound up with my house, as well as a slew of other stories about the neighborhood. He also mentioned that if it got really hot, we could call him to use his pool.

Never again would I think of him as "the guy who parks his expensive car so that it takes up two spaces." He was now my neighbor. Two weeks later, I found an opportune moment to slip into our conversation an observation about how "three cars can fit on the street if we pull up to the edge of the driveways." Bingo: My parking problem was fixed, plus I now had an ally in the neighborhood.

Over the next month or so, the other renters in my building and I got to know our neighbors. Having grown up in the country, I never fully realized how helpful neighbors can be. Mr. Greenford, a lawyer, gave us tips on how to handle our landlord, traffic tickets, noise violations—all

HEADS UP: NEIGHBORLY FAVORS

There will probably come a time when you need to ask a favor of a neighbor. You might be leaving on vacation, for example, and so you ask, "Say, Mrs. Nextdoor, I was wondering if I could ask you for a favor. Would you mind stopping by to feed my cat for a week? I'll be out of town from the tenth to the seventeenth, and my roommate will be gone too. . . . Are you sure? . . . Thank you so much. He just needs a cup of dry food each day and fresh water. You don't need to worry about the litter box. Thanks again!"

When you ask a favor, always make it clear that you'll gladly reciprocate anytime: "If there's anything I can ever do, you know all you have to do is ask!" Also, look for some way to express your thanks. If a neighbor is checking on your place while you're away, send a postcard from wherever you're traveling, thanking them; then bring a gift from your destination to give them when you get back, along with a handwritten note of thanks. Your neighbor will feel appreciated and will be more than ready to help you out again.

the useful stuff. The Clifftons, on the other side of us, had lived in the neighborhood for almost 50 years. Mrs. Cliffton swore she'd never call the cops on us "poor college kids" because the noise violations were just too expensive (we loved her!). Mr. and Mrs. Hyde, across the street, had two sons our age and a dog, who loved to hang out on our porch. The Cormets, next door to them, were always willing to lend us gardening tools, and their son worked at my favorite restaurant. (He helped me out one night when I forgot my ID.)

FOUR STEPS TO NEIGHBORHOOD PEACE

Whether you live in a residential neighborhood of freestanding houses, a condo development, or a tall apartment building, it's always to your benefit to get to know your neighbors. Unfortunately, many people fear having young people in their late teens or early twenties living next door—assuming that it automatically means noise, late-night parties, and messy lawns. The solution? Get to know your neighbors—and allay their fears about you—through a few simple actions:

1. *Introduce yourself as soon as possible after you move in.* Instead of viewing your neighbors from afar, never getting close enough to discover who they really are—or to let them know who you are—make it a point to introduce yourself at the first opportunity that presents itself. How hard is it to just say hello? "Hi, I'm Lizzie, I just moved in next door."

2. *Give your neighbors your phone number.* This gesture helps cement a bond. It's a sign of trust, an invitation to communicate, and an implicit promise to stay connected. *Wait a*

minute! you're thinking; *I don't want some old coot calling me up night and day.* Don't worry: The nutty busybody next door is the exception, not the rule. And if there's ever a problem—say, your party gets a bit louder than you realized—your neighbors will be ten times more likely to call you rather than your landlord or, worse yet, the police, if they have your phone number handy. And they won't have it handy unless you give it to them.

3. **When you have a loud party (or a band rehearsal or jam session or whatever), tell your neighbors in advance.** "I wanted to let you know we're having a 'just moved in' barbecue on Friday night. You're more than welcome to come over. I thought I'd tell you because we usually stay up pretty late at these things—so if we're too loud, just give us the word and we'll tone it down. Take care!"

4. **Smile at your neighbors.** So simple, so easy, and so important. Everyone enjoys a smile—so why not send one your neighbor's way? They may or may not smile back, but don't let that stop you. If they're not into reciprocating, that's their problem, not yours.

WHAT MAKES A GOOD NEIGHBOR?

To a great degree, how well you get along with your neighbors will depend on your neighbors and what their standards of behavior are. Some things are clearly out of bounds—putting garbage out without securing it properly, leaving trash lying around, failing to clean up after your dog, failing to return a borrowed item, or playing loud music late at night.

INSTANT TIP

I f you borrow a tool or piece of equipment from a neighbor, it's up to you to return the item promptly in the condition that you got it in. If the item breaks or is damaged while in your care, it's your obligation either to get it repaired or replace it with a new one. It doesn't matter if that shovel was ancient and ready to snap at any minute or if the leaf blower had never been properly maintained—whatever happens on your watch is your responsibility.

On other issues, like how well you tend your yard or whether you hang laundry out to dry, the line between considerate and inconsiderate behavior often depends on local custom.

Case in point: Christina had a difficult time adjusting to the demands of her new neighborhood. At her old apartment, she and her roommates always left their sweaty gym clothes outside to air dry before putting them in their laundry bags. It never bothered their neighbors one bit (or if it did, they never mentioned it). So when Christina moved to her new neighborhood, she did her usual thing, hanging out her gym clothes on the back porch where they wouldn't be visible from the street.

The next morning, she woke up to a note on her door:

You need to clean up your back porch. It's an absolute eyesore! Dirty clothes, boxes, and recycling! I don't want to look at it!
Your Neighbor, #34

Not wanting to pick a fight or get into a philosophical discussion about neighborly conduct, she cleaned up the entire back porch. "I guess this neighborhood is different," she told a friend later.

WHEN YOU'RE THE ONE WHO NEEDS TO SPEAK UP

Besides keeping your ears open for neighborly complaints or possible problems, it's also important to make your own needs and wishes known to your neighbors. If you're the one who is being offended or disturbed, or if you're concerned about a borrowed item that hasn't been returned, here are some ways to broach the subject:

"Do you have a minute, Mrs. Nextdoor? I wanted to talk, but if this is a bad time, we can do it later." If she replies, Yes, what is it? then continue . . . *"I was just concerned about the parking situation. You see, I leave for work at six in the morning, and Mr. Nextdoor's car always seems to jut out just enough so that I have to drive up on the curb to get out of my driveway. Would you mind if I put a stake up at the corner, so that he can see how far to pull up?"*

"Hi, Miss Downthestreet! I'm planning on raking the yard this afternoon, and I was wondering if I could come by and pick up my rake from you."

When you have a neighbor who isn't so considerate, your goal should always be to resolve the situation without harming the relationship. Staying as calm and polite as you possibly can in all encounters, including any discussions of problematic behavior, will go a long way toward accomplishing this goal.

ASK LIZZIE: SHOULD I CALL THE COPS?

Q: The guys living next door throw parties from time to time, and their last few have been *really* loud and have gone *really* late. I don't know them very well, and I feel uncomfortable confronting them about it. The next time they have a party that lasts beyond one in the morning, would I be out of line if I called the police to come ask them to quiet down?

LIZZIE: There are times when your absolute last resort—calling the police—is your only option. However, you should turn to this option only when the situation is untenable, unsafe, or someone is likely breaking the law.

Your first step, ideally, should be to try and talk the problem over with your neighbors. Of course, this isn't always practical. You might feel uncomfortable dealing directly with these particular neighbors (as in your case), or communication may simply be impossible.

Trevor ran into exactly this sort of problem with an overly excitable neighbor of his. Trevor's apartment had a back porch that faced the neighbor's bedroom window. Trevor liked hanging out on the porch in nice weather, but whenever he did, the neighbor called the police to file a noise complaint, even if Trevor was just talking and he could see that there was no party or disturbance of any kind—just two people sitting on the porch chatting. After several such incidents, the police finally asked the neighbor to stop calling.

When *should* you get the authorities involved? If you're dealing with a relatively minor issue such as a barking dog or trash that isn't secured properly, most cities have a city official with whom you can lodge a complaint rather than call the police. The time to call the cops is when you or others may be *harmed by someone* or if you're facing a *legitimate, enforceable disturbance*. In the case of your partying neighbors, if the noise is repeatedly disturbing you and others during normal sleeping hours or if you think there's a potential for violence to break out, then by all means make the call.

CHAPTER 5

WELCOME TO MY HOME:

HANGING OUT, THE ETIQUETTE OF COUCH CRASHING, AND HOW TO BE THE IDEAL HOUSEGUEST

ONE OF THE GREAT THINGS about living on your own is that you can have your friends over anytime you want. There's one catch: if you have roommates, your friends aren't coming over to just your house; they're coming to your roommates' house as well. Remember those skills of communication, compromise and commitment? Great—because you'll need them here. Whether you're chilling with friends while your roommate is trying to study, or your roommate's Significant Other is staying over for the fourth night in a row, or your sofa bed is taken up by a couple of out-of-town friends who haven't said exactly how long they plan on staying, when it comes to hosting (or being) a houseguest, everyone has to be on the same page for it to work. Otherwise, you're asking for trouble.

HANGING OUT AT HOME: SETTING THE GROUND RULES

We all have our own, unique social lives, and as newly independents we're in the process of developing new relationships and forging new friendships. If you're planning to live with roommates, it's always a good idea to negotiate some ground rules for having friends over *before* you actually move in together. I know, I know: Rules are a drag. I thought so, too—until I experienced firsthand just how essential they can be to maintaining a happy home life.

I'm a pretty sociable person. But when I lived with Christina, I was in a hermit phase. I simply didn't have a huge social life at that time: Most of my friends were abroad, I was in a long-distance relationship, and my course load had gone from nil to very heavy in the space of one semester.

Christina, on the other hand, had just left dorm life for off-campus housing, and the majority of her friends were still living in dorm rooms. I knew that a swarm of her dorm friends would be irresistibly drawn to our so-called authority-free apartment. The problem in a nutshell: Our social lives were drastically different, and our living room was very small. So Christina and I sat down and talked about the situation. Here are the issues we considered, the rules we agreed upon, and *why*:

Maximum Occupancy Allowed

Rule 1: If one of us was planning to have more than three people over to our apartment, we had to talk it over with the other roommate first.

Why? Our space was limited—and if, like me, you're planning to settle in for a quiet night at home and seven of your roommate's friends are commandeering the living room, things can get a little overwhelming.

The Right to Study Freely

Rule 2: *If one of us was studying, she shouldn't have to leave the apartment to find peace and quiet. (Some people choose the opposite rule: If you need to study, go to the library.)*

Why? We both felt that work came before play and that friends can always hang out anywhere—whereas a place to concentrate and focus can be more difficult to come by.

Communicating About Workload

Rule 3: *If one of us had a test or a big paper due, we should inform the other roommate in advance, so that any socializing could be done outside the apartment.*

Why? Making it known ahead of time that you're going to need a night of peace and quiet can help offset feelings of resentment and

BE HONEST ABOUT YOUR OWN FEELINGS

If you bottle up your feelings about what's really bothering you, your frustration will continue to build. To avoid a regrettable blowup, air your concerns as soon as possible in a matter-of-fact, nonaccusatory way: "Hey, Sam, I found a bunch of my CDs scattered on the floor this morning. I don't mind if you and your friends listen to them, but if you put them back in their cases it'll keep them from getting scratched. Thanks."

avoid a possibly ugly confrontation. No one wants to have to yell at people to pipe down at 1 AM the night before an exam—or be the one getting yelled at, for that matter.

Veto Power

Rule 4: If one of us was on bad terms with a friend of a roommate, we agreed to inform the roommate of the uncomfortable feelings.

Why? Neither of us wanted to feel uncomfortable with a guest in our home. This didn't mean that the guest wasn't allowed over—just that we would try to have that person over only when our roommate was out.

Cleaning Up

Rule 5: Whoever had friends over had to clean up the place afterward—before he or she left the house. Sometimes this meant doing dishes; sometimes it meant just getting them into the sink. Always it meant straightening up the living room.

Why? Neither of us felt that it was fair to leave our roommate to deal with our mess while we were out having a good time.

OVERNIGHT OR WEEKEND VISITORS

Hosting overnight guests is another enjoyable aspect of having your own place. But overnighters bring their own special challenges. Whether your guests are friends visiting for the weekend, an acquaintance crashing on the couch, or a significant other who has taken up semipermanent residence, you need to make your visitors feel welcome and comfortable in your home, while causing as little disturbance to the lifestyles of your roommates (and yourself) as possible.

THE GOOD HOST CHECKLIST

To ensure that your guests' overnight stay is comfortable for everyone . . .

— If they've never been to your home, make sure your guests have directions to your apartment or house.

— Welcome your guests when they arrive and show them around the house, including where they'll be sleeping, where to stow their belongings, and in general which stuff belongs to you (and therefore is theirs to use at your discretion) and which is your roommate's (and therefore shouldn't be used without asking).

— Give your guests a heads-up on basics such as when your roommate will be coming or going, your own schedule, and anything else pertaining to how the house operates. Definitely let them know what is and isn't off-limits in the fridge.

— Provide your guests with clean towels, and make sure their sleeping area has clean sheets and blankets, a pillow with a clean pillow case, a box of tissues, and a good light.

— Make sure the bathroom has fresh soap and a new roll of toilet paper—and that an additional roll is handy in the cabinet.

Explaining Daily Routines

Fill your guests in on your household routine: "We all generally sleep in on Sunday, so if you get up early, just hit the start button on the coffeemaker and help yourself to the cereal in the cabinet." If your roommate has an early class or has to go to work in the morning, inform your guest. That way, he or she will know to keep quiet and to stay out of the shower until the roommate has left for the morning.

HEADS UP: THE LIVING ROOM IS *NOT* ANOTHER BEDROOM

 ecause the living room is communal space, friends who crash overnight on the couch have to respect the house's waking hours. Basically, it's the obligation of the couch crasher to wake up when the rest of the household does. In addition, sometimes you just have to say no. If it's an inconvenient time to have someone sleep on the sofa—for instance, you have to make some business calls from home the next morning—it's perfectly okay to tell the would-be crasher that tonight's not a good night.

Frequent Overnighters

The frequent guest has more responsibility than an occasional guest to blend in with the household, particularly if the guest is a boyfriend or girlfriend, in which case they have quasi-roommate status (see "Significant Others," page 68). The frequent overnighter who adjusts his routine to the household's schedule is a pleasure, but little things like leaving toothbrushes, clothing, or towels strewn around the apartment can become annoyances to others in the house. Food is another potentially touchy issue. If you and your roommate have agreed to split the food bill, and his girlfriend tends to get the munchies late at night, the two of them should either make a point of re-stocking the snack supplies or offer to chip in some extra money for the grocery bill.

HOSTING LONG-TERM HOUSEGUESTS

If you plan on having a friend or relative visit for more than a night, *ask your roommates first.* I can't stress this enough. Tests, job interviews, personal issues—there are a multitude of reasons why it's important to discuss overnight guests with your roommates and get their okay long before any travel arrangements have been made.

Here are some other points to consider before inviting a long-term houseguest:

- **It's okay to say no.** The first step in handling issues with long-term guests is to carefully consider who you allow to stay long-term in your apartment. It's absolutely fine to refuse a request. You can simply say, "I'm sorry; my apartment just isn't a good place to stay long term." You really don't need to explain. Any good friend—or anybody with an ounce of consideration, for that matter—will understand.

- **Set firm start and end dates for the visit.** The visit should last only as long as you plan on it lasting, so discuss up front exactly when your guests will be arriving, and exactly how long they intend to stay. "Surprise—I'm staying an extra week!" can be really stressful on your roommates—not to mention on you.

- **Find out what's going on in your roommate's life.** Is there an important day in your roommate's life that falls during your guest's visit—such as a birthday or an anniversary she'd like to celebrate? Although your roommate may still say it's fine for you to have a houseguest, there may be nights when you and your

HOUSEGUEST SNAFUS AND HOW TO HANDLE THEM

OOPS	FIX IT NOW	NEXT TIME
Guest eats room-mate's food	Your guest prob-ably didn't realize the food was off-limits. You should replace the room-mate's food.	Let your guest know the situation and what food is okay to eat.
Guest ditches host	Find your friend and explain the importance of his visit to you—or let him go on his merry way.	Find out if your guest wants to visit you or the town. This way you'll know what to expect.
Guest borrows something with-out asking	Explain that the item wasn't meant to be loaned and that the guest needs to return it.	Let your guest know you and your roommates' bor-rowing policies.
Guest breaks something	Hopefully, he or she will offer to replace it. If not, ask them if they would split the cost with you.	It happens: things break. If you're really attached to something, stow it away in a safe place.

CONTINUED

OOPS	FIX IT NOW	NEXT TIME
Guest gripes to your roommates about the noise they're making	Apologize to your roommates, and explain to your guest that it's their apartment as well.	Explain house schedules to your guest so that he or she understands from the start when people will be up and about.
Guest uses phone to make expensive phone calls	If they ask, request that they reimburse you. If they don't, call and explain the circumstances and ask for a reimbursement.	Politely request that your guest not make such calls without using a credit or calling card or calling collect.
Guest is a slob	Create Cleaning Day: Explain to your guest that you and roommate regularly clear up clutter and suggest a job for the guest to do.	Explain the level of mess you and your roommate can comfortably handle before a long-term guest comes to stay.

guest will need to plan your comings and goings around your roommate's activities.

- *Discuss expenses with your roommates and your guest.* When you have a houseguest coming to stay for two weeks and that houseguest will be putting away three square meals a day plus snacks—well, you do the math. I'm guessing that being young and independent, you don't have the cash to supply a houseguest with two weeks' worth of food. If your guest is planning to stay for an extended period, unless you've offered to foot the bill for your guest, you have every right to ask him or her to chip in on expenses like groceries and any food you order in. What you don't want is a long-term freeloader eating you out of house and home. So again, lay out the ground rules up front with both your roommate and your houseguest.

- *Don't forget about the landlord.* Believe it or not, many landlords do notice houseguests. If your landlord has a watchful eye, you may want to check your lease to see if it limits the consecutive days a nontenant is allowed to stay in the building without paying rent. I've seen at least one lease that limited the presence of a houseguest to fourteen days. So check to be sure, rather than risk getting a surprise call from your landlord.

INSTANT TIP

I f you know ahead of time that your guest will be staying at your place long term, consider letting her crash in your bedroom. The living room can often be too public a place for one person to occupy for more than a few days.

ASK LIZZIE: FRIEND OR FREELOADER?

Q: Help! A friend of mine has been crashing in the living room of my new apartment for a week now and shows no sign of leaving anytime soon. He just says he wants to "check out the city." How do I politely ask him to hit the road so I can have my place (and my life) back?

LIZZIE: This is a classic example of why you should *always* pin down the starting and ending dates of any visit at the time you're setting it up. Extending an open-ended invitation ("Sure, stay at my place as long as you like!") is just asking for trouble. Since that's the situation you're stuck in, however, your best approach is to make it clear to your friend that while you've enjoyed the visit, you'll be needing to get back your regular schedule soon. If necessary, mention a specific date and time: "I'm going to be starting a tough new work assignment on Monday morning. I'll really need to have the living room free by then, so I can use it as a home office."

If your friend still balks at leaving, offer to find him alternate accommodations: "I'd be glad to check out the rates at the Downtown Hotel—I think they're pretty reasonable. And there's also a youth hostel around the corner . . ." From the sound of things, the prospect of paying for accommodations should be enough to light a fire under your friend.

When issues with long-term houseguests do crop up, they have to be faced directly. It's hard to do, I know, but if your guest's actions are causing problems with your roommates or yourself, you have to be honest and explain to your guest what's going on. If talking doesn't resolve the problem, it may be necessary to ask your guest to leave.

Finally, once the guest has gone, write your roommate a thank-you note for agreeing to let your guest stay for so long. Trust me, your roommate will appreciate your recognition of the fact that it can be a strain to accommodate a guest for so long—especially when the guest is your friend, not theirs.

LEAVING TOWN? DON'T PULL A "TIM"

Imagine coming home on a Friday afternoon, psyched that the weekend is finally here and even more psyched because your roommate is going away. The house is all yours—or at least there's one less person around. Then you walk into the kitchen to find a pile of dishes packed into the sink. *Oh, great,* you think. Next, you check the phone messages: "Hey, guys, it's Bill, your landlord. I'll be by the house tomorrow. Tim, I'll need your part of the rent—so have it ready."

Way to go, Tim! You've gone off and left a mess of problems for your roommates to deal with.

When you leave your apartment for vacation or even for the weekend, please don't pull a "Tim." To guarantee that your roommates are happy and your homecoming is an enjoyable one:

1. Let your roommates know in advance when you'll be leaving and when you will be returning.

2. Plan on setting aside some time before you go to clean up a bit.

   a. *Kitchen:* Wash any dishes, and throw away your leftovers or food that might spoil while you're gone.
   b. *Bathroom:* Put away any of your stuff that you're not taking with you.
   c. *Living room:* Clear away your clutter (dump it in your room if you don't have time to put it away), straighten up, and, if you can, vacuum.

3. Check with your roommates about any bills or rent that needs paying.

4. If you plan to be gone for more than a week or two, you may want to discuss temporarily modifying your financial arrangements: After all, you won't be there to eat the food, so you don't really need to chip in on the week's grocery bill, right?

Of course, responsibility swings both ways. If it's *you* who's going on vacation, know that you have every right to expect to return to a clean, financially stable home. I loved living with Christina, especially because I knew that whenever I went away, I'd come back home to a clean apartment. The living room would have been straightened and vacuumed; the bathroom would be clean; there'd be no clothes on the floor, hair in the drain, or globs of toothpaste in the sink. The dishes were always done, and sometimes the drying rack would have been emptied! There was plenty of room for me to unpack and relax without having to clean up the common areas first.

If you find yourself in this happy situation, show your appreciation for the fact that your roommate cleaned for your return. Comment on how nice the place looks and how thankful you are for her efforts. We all crave a little gratitude—and appreciation becomes an incentive for the next time.

WHEN YOU'RE THE GUEST

The first thing to understand about hanging out at a friend's apartment or house is that people can be very particular about their home environments. Always remember that you are in someone else's home and be respectful of that space, as well as of the belongings and people in it.

INSTANT TIP

I f you plan on visiting a friend for more than two days, take your host and his or her housemates out to dinner one night as an expression of thanks. If this is beyond your budget, offer to buy groceries and prepare a meal at home one evening. Even cleaning up when your host is at work or out is a thoughtful gesture of thanks.

The Etiquette of Hanging Out

Steve spent a good deal of time hanging out at his friend Tina's apartment, which she shared with two other girls. Steve always made a point of doing several things that made it really pleasant to have him over:

- He always engaged Tina's roommates in conversation, asking them how they were doing, what they'd been up to, and so on. When you are visiting a friend, it's important to acknowledge your friend's roommates and include them in any conversation. Who knows? You may gain a new friend.

- People often drop by for a quick *what's up*, sometimes with unannounced mini-entourages in tow—which can be a little disconcerting for the people who suddenly find their apartment flooded with half a dozen new friends. Steve always gave Tina and her housemates plenty of advance warning if he was planning on bringing other people along with him.

- Before Steve left, not only did he always ask Tina and her roommates what he could do to clean up, but then he actually pitched in and helped. This was a huge deal to them, because so few of their friends ever did this. *Big tip*: By all means, relax and enjoy your visit—but at the same time, remember to respect your hosts' home life, and *offer to help clean up.* Better yet, just pitch in and do it.

The Etiquette of Couch Crashing

There's an unspoken catch to crashing on the couch or floor, especially if you're crashing in a living room that people have to pass through to get to other shared spaces such as the kitchen or the bathroom: If your slumber is disturbed, you don't get to complain about it or ask the resident noisemaker to quiet down. Why? *Because it's not your home.* (How shocked would *you* be if you woke up to some stranger sleeping on your couch, only to hear him grumble, as you walk into your kitchen to get breakfast, "Could you *please* keep it down?") On the flip side, you're also obligated not to disturb the resident sleepers, and regardless of whether you leave early or late (or how well you sleep), you should also straighten up the couch and the area around it before you go.

The Overnight Houseguest

If you're just crashing on someone's couch after a night out, you don't really need to do much beyond getting up on time, tidying up, and saying thank you. If you've been formally invited to stay over at a friend's

WHEN IN ROME . . .

Whenever I've visited friends, I've always found that the best approach is to take my cues from them. I watch what they do in terms of cleanup, eating, and noise levels. If my friend is whispering as we approach the door at night, I'm guessing we should be quiet. If he takes off his shoes, so will I. If he washes the dishes after dinner, I'll help clean up, too.

place, however, your houseguest etiquette needs to be stepped up a notch. Here are some key points to remember:

- *Always bring a gift.* The cardinal rule for all invited overnight guests is that they should arrive carrying a house gift. It doesn't have to be expensive—a bottle of wine, some homemade or bought food, a little piece of artwork, heck, even something fun or goofy like a Slinky will do fine. The point is, you're giving your hosts some token of your gratitude that says "Thank you for welcoming me into your home."

- *Offer to chip in on expenses,* especially if you're staying more than one night. Being young and independent, it's rare that we are able to afford to eat out every meal, and it's asking a lot to have your friends pay for everything you consume in their home. Rather than wait for them to mention it, beat your hosts to the punch by offering up front to contribute to the purchase of groceries and other supplies.

- *Always bring your own toiletries* (toothbrush, hairbrush, deodorant, shaving materials) instead of expecting your host to supply them.

- *Tidy up after yourself,* especially in the bathroom, kitchen, and living area.

- *Offer to help out* by running errands, doing household chores, and pitching in with the food preparation and cleanup.

- *Let your host know if you make other plans* during your visit, and invite him or her along if it's appropriate. ("I've arranged to grab dinner with Anne on Thursday night. If you don't have any plans, would you like to join us?")

TEN HOUSE GIFT IDEAS

- Candles
- Houseplant
- Flowers
- Hand towels
- Place mats
- Book
- CD of a favorite musician
- DVD of a favorite movie
- Bottle of wine or liqueur
- Specialty food (freshly ground coffee, bakery goods for breakfast, chocolates, etc.)

- *Offer to cover the cost of anything you accidentally damage.* If the item is way out of your price range—an expensive lamp, for example—then offer to pay whatever you can. As long as you make the *attempt* to help out, your kind gesture will go a long way toward replacing the ruined item.

- *As you're leaving, thank your friend and your friend's housemates* for allowing you to stay. Leaving a note with a bottle of wine or a bouquet of flowers is a really nice gesture and will leave a lasting, favorable impression. Who wouldn't want to have you back again?

- *Follow up by sending a thank-you note in the mail.* Or, better yet, send something even more tangible. When my boyfriend visited my best friend in San Diego to check out the city, he knew her birthday was coming up soon. So when he got back, instead of just sending a thank-you note, he sent her flowers as well. She was blown away.

THE LONG-TERM HOUSEGUEST

Whenever you stay with friends for longer than a week or two, you've surpassed the "houseguest" level and have become, for all intents and purposes, a temporary tenant. Not only should you offer to chip in on food expenses (or even start buying groceries on your own), but you should also offer to chip in on other household bills, like utilities and cable TV. It's also important that you clean up after yourself at all times and make indications of your presence (sleeping area, belongings, etc.) as unobtrusive as possible. Finally, discuss with your hosts their feelings about your inviting your friends over to their place—and always give them advance warning if you do.

Whether you're a housemate or a houseguest, you can never go wrong as long as you *remember the core principles of etiquette*. If your actions are guided by consideration, respect, and honesty, you're virtually guaranteed that any visit will go smoothly.

CHAPTER 6

SIGNIFICANT OTHERS, ONE-NIGHT STANDS, AND THINGS THAT GO BUMP IN THE NIGHT:

ROMANCE, DATING, AND SEX AT YOUR PLACE

ONE OF THE MAJOR revelations you'll have as a newly independent living with other newly independents is that people are unique and have wildly differing views and habits. You may think you've found the most compatible roommate in the world, only to discover that the person you're living with is a slob, a liar, or worse. But nothing, and I mean *nothing*, can reveal differences among housemates the way love and sex can.

Keep in mind that everyone is coming into this new living situation from a unique emotional place. Some people may have just ended a relationship; others are desperate to be in one. Some are only interested in one-night stands, some don't approve of sex before marriage, and others couldn't care less about sex.

It's hard enough for new housemates to adjust to living with one another without throwing a significant other (or even a one-night stand) into the mix. Handling these issues can be a very touchy matter—and one that not everyone agrees on. This is why you should talk to your roommates early on to determine their comfort level with boyfriends, girlfriends, sex, and one-night stands.

Whether you're in a relationship of a year or a night, sharing time and space with your sweetie at your place has the potential to be a burden on other roommates. If the privilege is abused—say, the love interest is invading everyone's personal space, hanging out and not helping out, becoming a financial drag, or even being crude or offensive (or, worse yet, monopolizing the TV)—then the other housemates have every right to kick your sweetie's butt to the curb.

Having a love interest around can also foment jealousy and resentment in others—hey, we're all human, and we just wanna be loved!—and the considerate roommate is one who doesn't flaunt his or her relationship at the expense of others.

Because serious relationships raise different issues than do casual flings, and because the etiquette of having sex in a shared house is a whole issue unto itself, I've broken this chapter into three sections: *significant others*, *one-night stands*, and *things that go bump in the night*.

SIGNIFICANT OTHERS

If you have a significant other who you know will be spending a good deal of time at your place, here are a few things to consider before the lovefest begins:

- Above all, *consider your roommate's feelings and beliefs*. No matter how discreet you are, your love life will have an effect on your roommate. The period when you're first embarking on a relationship is a good time to have a talk with your roommate(s), and ask what their thoughts are about your sweetie coming over or spending the night.

- If you and your significant other spend a considerable amount of time together at your place, you'll need to *take into account over-lapping food and utility consumption*—not to mention space consumption. Check with your roommate(s) and your sweetheart on an ongoing basis to make sure that food, bills, and living space don't become an issue. Chipping in extra for expenses can help, but if your roommate(s) are feeling cramped by your love life, you and your S.O. may need to consider lowering your relationship profile a bit on the home front and maybe spending a little more time at sweetie's place instead. Remember, your roommate(s) have signed on to live with *you,* not your S.O.

- Bear in mind that *you are still responsible for your guest,* even if your guest is your significant other who is there on a regular basis. Hopefully, your S.O. is considerate enough to clean up his messes at your house, but ultimately his messes (or any other potentially thorny issues) are *your* responsibility.

ONE-NIGHT STANDS

It's one thing when your S.O. is hanging around your place, since he or she is really part of the extended family, so to speak. Bringing home someone you just met that night, though, is another deal entirely. That's why it's best to set up house rules at the very start about whether it's cool to allow a stranger to sleep over.

For one thing, inviting any new person into your house overnight carries a certain risk. I wish it weren't so, but the reality is that people

WHEN YOU'RE THE ONE STAYING OVER

I f you're the significant other who's staying over, you have certain responsibilities to your sweetie and to your hosts. Always keep in mind the following:

• **ACKNOWLEDGE YOUR SWEETIE'S ROOMMATES.** Don't treat them as if they're invisible—after all, you're staying in their home! You don't have to be best friends with your S.O.'s roommates, but you should attempt to establish some kind of relationship with them. Acknowledging them politely and engaging in conversation is a great way to get the acquaintanceship off on the right foot. And let's face it—" 'Sup?" sounds very different from, "Hey, Karen, how's it going?"

• **HELP OUT.** If you spend a lot of time at your significant other's place, you should be making every effort to help out in the household. Taking out the trash, washing the dishes, fixing something that's broken, and cleaning up any mess you make will be very much appreciated. If you want to go the extra mile, offer to cook dinner for your sweetie and housemates. Just filling a vase with fresh flowers can endear you to the hardest-hearted housemate. And of course, whenever you depart, thank your hosts for their hospitality.

• **DON'T HOG THE TV, DVD, OR CD PLAYER.** A no-brainer, right? Still, you'd be surprised at the number of freeloaders who take advantage of household entertainment systems. Want to spend a nice Sunday afternoon taking in a game on the tube? Sorry: Your girlfriend's roommates are recovering from the night before by watching Brad Pitt, and it's their television, their apartment, and their choice. Unless you're helping to pay their cable bill, you shouldn't be monopolizing or complaining about the TV.

aren't always as trustworthy as they seem. When one roommate and I lived together, we never discussed the issue of strangers staying the night. One night she met this cute European guy and his friend at a bar, and they followed us home. She entertained while I, suffering from the effects of one drink too many, paid homage to the porcelain god in the bathroom and then headed straight for bed.

Once under the covers, I called my boyfriend to tell him what a rotten night I'd had. As I was talking to him on the phone, my door swung open—and there, lo and behold, stood Euro Guy's friend, attempting to sleep in my room rather than on the couch. Needless to say, my hero made it to my place in about two seconds flat. My

THE ETIQUETTE OF SEX FOR ONE NIGHT

So you've brought someone home for one night. What are the rules for this? No matter how casual the encounter may be, etiquette still plays a role:

First, both visitor and host need to determine whether staying the night is in the cards at all. If either of them doesn't feel comfortable turning it into a sleepover, it's best to make this clear up front in a tactful way: "I have an early meeting tomorrow, so I think it's best if you didn't stay . . ." If the visitor does sleep over, the two of you are under no obligation whatsoever to exchange phone numbers, go to breakfast together, and so on. Do, however, show your guest to the door when it's time to leave (especially if this means traveling past a gauntlet of roommates)—or, better yet, walk the other person out to the street.

Finally, if you slip out of the house before the other person wakes up (let's face it, this does happen), be sure to leave a note.

roommate, meanwhile, was furious that someone she'd brought home would have a friend crass enough to try to sleep with a sick roommate.

Bottom line: We both learned that bringing people home—even if they intend to sleep on the couch—isn't always safe.

With that caveat out of the way, one-night stands can be fun for everyone, provided you watch out for a couple of key points:

- *Be considerate of the sleeping.* Since most one-night stands seem to happen at night, you'll need to take extra care not to disturb others. Try to be as quiet as you can when coming in for the evening. Explain to your guest that you have roommates sleeping and you don't want to wake them.

- *Heads up (no pun intended).* There's nothing like waking up to go to the bathroom and, in a state of grogginess, walking in on a total stranger while both of you are in your underwear. Remember, to your roommates, your conquest might look like a burglar using the bathroom! To get around this potentially dangerous scenario, you'll need to find some way to let your roommates know you have a guest who will probably still be here in the morning.

  One good solution is to slip your roommates a note under their doors. You can also come up with some kind of signal. I know two guys who set up a system to let each other know when a late-night guest was in the house. If one of them had a guest for the night, he would put shoes immediately outside the other guy's door. This way, when the roommate stumbled out of his room in a fog, he'd trip over the shoes, which he knew meant there was a guest in the house. (Apparently, a note was too subtle in their case.)

THINGS THAT GO BUMP
IN THE NIGHT

Thud. Moan. Thud. Moan. Thud. Moan.

The first time I heard those noises coming from the room next door, I thought, *Well, I can either bang on the wall and be ticked off about the clamor, or I can sit here embarrassed, or I can think, Damn, good for you!*

One of the great things about being independent is that you get to go bump in the night. But if you live with other people, the pragmatic reality is that you can't just go bump in the night (or day) willy-nilly. It's always smart to do your bumping responsibly and respectfully and use discretion and consideration for others. For starters, try to keep the fun in your bedroom. No one wants to imagine you've been going at it on the kitchen table or on the living-room couch. Also, if you like to shower with your sweetie, keep in mind that sounds carry, especially in the bathroom.

What if you live with extremely thin walls? If you've already agreed that it's okay to bring home significant others or one-night stands, then the other roommates will have to come up with a system for dealing with it, such as buying earplugs, turning up the music, or simply being happy for the roommate who got lucky.

When it comes to sex at home, there are two simple guidelines:

- **Talk to your potential roommates about it—then keep talking once you've moved in together.** I began this chapter by mentioning how important it is to discuss everyone's tolerance for sexual activity in the house before deciding to share your living space with other people. Once you've moved in together, you need to continue keeping the lines of communication open. When Christina and I lived together, I asked her to

please let me know if anything ever bothered her in that department, because I never wanted to make her feel uncomfortable
in her own home. Even in close quarters, something can usually
be worked out: Unless you're a real exhibitionist, you can always
find ways to keep the noise within respectful limits. On the
other hand, you may discover that as far as the other person is
concerned, *anyone* having sex in the house is simply taboo. This
is *exactly* why you need to discuss the issue of sex *before* you
decide to room together.

- **Shut the door.** Sophie, this one's for you: Having been temporarily "scarred for life" after seeing two of her roommates going
  bump midday with the door wide open, Sophie had one request
  when we moved in together—and I think it's a really good one
  for everybody: Shut the door.

CHAPTER 7

ENTERTAINING:

FROM WINE TASTING TO BEER PONG, AND EVERYTHING IN BETWEEN

Y OU'VE GOT YOUR own place, you've feng shui'd the whole apartment, and you've been having a great time hanging out with your friends in your new home. Now the moment has come to take your next big step: It's time to throw a party. Whether a dinner party, a cocktail party, or just a casual get-together with close friends, you'll want the people you invite into your home to have a great time. And hey, you want to show yourself a good time as well! But you also don't want to be overwhelmed. Fortunately, with a dash of planning (and a pinch of etiquette), you can make any affair go smoothly *and* guarantee that everyone will be panting to come back the next time you throw a bash.

NO MATTER WHO'S HOSTING WHAT

Regardless of what kind of party you're throwing, the idea is to bring together a group of people so that they can enjoy one another's company and feel welcome and happy in your home. Remember, as the host, you're in charge: People will be looking to you for guidance—so take on the role with gusto. You don't have to have fancy hors d'oeuvres or a killer band to have a good time; just stick to the following basic principles of party-giving, and your bash will be one to remember:

- Be sure to talk to each one of your guests at some point during the party.
- Keep an eye out to make sure everyone has all the drinks and food they need.
- Introduce guests who don't know each other.
- Make sure everyone is engaged and having a good time.

Believe it or not, it really is that simple. If you treat your guests like, well, *guests,* and shower them with good old-fashioned hospitality, the good vibrations will reverberate for weeks and months to come.

YOUR HOST WILL GREET YOU NOW

One of the biggest rookie mistakes a party-giver can make is not being ready and available when guests arrive. Nothing's worse than arriving at a party prepared to be entertained, only to find a frazzled host or hostess in serious need of helping hands. You'll want to be done with all the major party preparations *before* the first guest arrives. You don't want to be stuck in the kitchen cooking or running out to the store for last-minute supplies or still be getting dressed just as the party is getting underway.

To make sure this never happens, all you need to do is follow this Get-It-Together Party Prep List.

Get-It-Together Party Prep List

1. *Plan, plan, plan in advance,* either on your own (if you're throwing the party yourself) or with your roommates or co-hosts (if it's a group effort). Are you planning to serve food? Then plot out the menu and a timetable to make sure it can all be prepared before the party begins. Want to throw a theme party, spruce up your place with flowers, or hand out special party favors? All decorations, door prizes, and other twists should be picked up and in place well ahead of time. Finally, make sure you have enough silverware and dishware to go around, and think about how you'll be serving the food—buffet style or prepared plate?

2. *Invite your guests.* Take a careful look at your available seating and space and consider how many people can comfortably fit into your home. When it comes to issuing the actual invitation, no matter how you do it—e-mail, phone, mailbox—

E-VITES

These days, it's become acceptable to send invitations by e-mail for all but the most formal types of events (such as weddings or black-tie affairs), and for good reason: Not only does e-mailing save on postage, but it makes it a snap to RSVP. To send an extra-special invitation, do an online search for "E-vite" Web sites that let you design and send customized e-mail invitations—often at no cost.

let your guests know the following information (without it, you might find yourself partying alone):

a. Date
b. Time
c. Place
d. Specifics (such as the formality of the party; whether it's a celebration for someone or a theme night; whether they should bring a dish or beverage, and if so, what)

You'll also want to ask your guests to RSVP (reply) so that you'll know who and how many are coming—particularly if you're planning a small party, a dinner party, or a more formal party.

GIVE 'EM WARNING, MATE

W hether you send your invites by e-mail, mailbox, telephone, or text message, make sure that your guests have enough time to save the date. How far in advance should you send out your invitations? It depends on the type of gathering:

FOR . . .	ALLOW A LEAD TIME OF . . .
A small party with friends	Anywhere from when you first think of the idea up to the very last minute is okay.
An informal dinner	A few days to 3 weeks
A formal dinner	3 to 6 weeks
A cocktail party	2 to 4 weeks
An anniversary party	3 to 6 weeks
A bridal shower	3 to 6 weeks
A holiday party	1 month
A bon voyage party	From the last minute up to 3 weeks
A brunch	A few days to 2 weeks
Big bash	2 to 4 weeks

RSVP... PLEEEEASE!

You'll be glad to know that it's perfectly fine to call or e-mail your nonresponsive invitees to ask if they're coming or not. Just say something like, "I'm trying to get a handle on how many people are coming, and I wanted to see what your plans were." And the next time *you* receive an invitation, respond promptly.

3. *Pin down the menu.* The key here is to decide what type of food you want to serve (see "What Kind of Party Do You Want to Throw?" page 85), then stick to dishes you know how to cook and serve well and that can be prepared ahead of time. Remember, your role as the host or hostess is to make the effort seem effortless. You want to be able to relax and entertain your guests once they arrive, rather than be worried about what's cooking in the kitchen. It's also a good idea to find out what your guests might be allergic to (such as peanuts or shellfish, to name two common examples) and whether anyone is vegetarian or has other dietary needs. (This is particularly important if you're just having a few people over.) Once you've decided on your menu, review all the recipes in advance and collect all necessary ingredients.

4. *Stock up on beverages.* This may include sodas, juices, wine, beer, liquor—whatever you choose. Don't skimp: Your budget may not allow for a fully stocked bar, but wine, beer, and non-alcoholic drinks won't break the bank—and you're hosting a party, remember? Finally, don't forget the ice, and have plenty of glasses or cups on hand.

~ ASK LIZZIE: SHOULD I BRING SOMETHING?

Q: What should I say when guests call and ask if they should bring something?

LIZZIE: Unless you're hosting a potluck dinner or a BYOB party, a polite host doesn't ask her guests to bring anything. When someone calls to ask what they can bring, say, "Thank you so much—but really, you don't need to bring anything." If they persist, that's a signal for you to relent and suggest something that's not too expensive. "A bottle of either white or red wine would be fine—thanks!" (Even if you don't suggest anything, you'll find that some guests will show up with a little something anyway.)

5. *Clean up your place,* even if it's only your best friend coming over, before inviting guests into your home.

   - *Straighten the living room:* Clear away clutter, such as shoes, books, clothing; vacuum the floor; dust the tables.

   - *Take on the kitchen:* Sweep and/or mop the floor; clean the counters; put away dishes. Clean up as you cook, too: When you have an entire meal ready and the kitchen doesn't look like a disaster area, now *that's* time for celebrating. And make sure to take out the trash before your guests arrive.

   - *Tidy up the bathroom:* Clean around the sink, sweep or mop the floor, and scrub the toilet; make sure toilet paper is stocked and the wastebasket emptied. Put a nice bar of soap by the sink (this is a great opportunity to use those smelly bars of soap you swiped from your last hotel stay), and provide hand towels for guests to use.

⟋ INSTANT TIP ⟍

Ⓜ y mom always kept a container of extra tampons and pads in the house for emergencies. As a guest, there's nothing more embarrassing than getting your period when you're unprepared.

- *Finally, straighten up your bedroom* and make sure your bed is made and your dirty clothes are in the hamper. Even if you aren't using the bed as a coatrack, you never know who might glance in on their way to the bathroom—and if your guests are numerous and your place is small, your room may end up being a place where people hang out.

6. *Give yourself plenty of time to get ready.* Is it just me, or is it kinda awkward to sit in someone else's home as a just-arrived guest, watching while your host or hostess runs between the bathroom and the bedroom trying to get dressed and groomed? Plan on being dressed and ready and putting the finishing touches on your food, drinks, and decorating

⟋ SCAN FOR THE SCANDALOUS ⟍

Ⓨ our friends may love to read your racier magazines when they come over, but your S.O.'s parents probably won't care to. And while that awesome beer bottle collection on the mantel might get high marks from your college pals, your boss or work colleagues may be less than impressed. Before entertaining, do a clean sweep to make sure any questionable items are stowed safely away. There are some things people just don't want to see.

(even lighting candles!) in plenty of time to greet your guests when they arrive—as if this little shindig was a snap to put together.

MAKING THE "WALLFLOWER" WELCOME

When you're the host and you've got a hundred things to do, it's all too easy to overlook the guests you don't know as well. But as the host, it's your responsibility to greet any newcomers, introduce them to the group, and make sure they're mixing and having a good time with the other guests.

I had a great experience recently: Faced with friends leaving town for the summer, I was trying to branch out and meet new people. So when my friend Brent invited me to a party at his house, I was psyched. On the night of the party, however, I chickened out. I called Brent to let him know I wasn't coming, pleading fatigue. Finally I admitted my real reason to him: I was afraid I wouldn't know anyone, and I knew from harsh experience how easy it is to become a wallflower in that situation.

Brent's response was brief and to the point: "Holy crap, that's lame," he said. "Come on over!" So I did. When I got there, Brent welcomed me, introduced me to several people, and immediately got me a drink. Throughout the party, he and his girlfriend, Marybeth, made a special effort to talk to me and include me in conversations. Their intent was to see that everyone had a good time and felt welcome—and they succeeded. Now *that's* what makes a great party.

WHEN YOUR GUESTS ARRIVE

Once your doorbell starts ringing, you want to be free to focus all of your attention on your incoming guests. This doesn't mean standing and chatting for 20 minutes with each new arrival; you're the host, after all, and you need to spread your hospitality around. But it does mean . . .

- Greeting each new guest

- Introducing each new guest to another partygoer

- Lingering long enough to help get a conversation going

Let's look at each step in turn.

- *Greeting your guests:* You should meet each guest at the door as he or she arrives. If you know them already, simply smile, make eye contact, and greet them ("Suzie, Kyle—great to see you! I'm so glad you could come"), and shake their hand (a firm grip and two or three pumps is fine—avoid the limp, "dead fish" shake, as well as the "bone-crusher") or give them a kiss or hug, depending on how well you know them. If you don't know the guest, introduce yourself during the handshake ("Hi, I'm Bill. It's nice to meet you").

- *Introducing your guests:* Next, show your guests into the room and introduce them to some of the other guests: "Suzie and Kyle, I'd like you to meet Debbie and Alex." Among friends, it generally doesn't matter who you introduce to whom. If one of the parties is significantly older than the other, however, it's considered polite to speak to the older person first when making

ASK LIZZIE: SMOKE ALARM

Q: How should I handle my friends who smoke? Some of them get insulted when I don't let them smoke in my apartment.

LIZZIE: It's perfectly okay to ask your guests not to smoke in your home. It's your home, and you make the rules. Rather than putting up "No Smoking" signs, however, just leave an ashtray or small can in a convenient spot outside where your guests can smoke comfortably, such as the porch, front steps, or backyard. When someone asks you if it's okay to smoke, you can direct them there.

If a guest lights up in your home without asking, it's completely appropriate to walk over and say something like, "Kristin, I'd prefer it if you smoke out on the porch. Thanks."

---

the introduction: "Aunt Jenny and Uncle Fred, I'd like to introduce my friends Kyle and Suzie."

- *Help get a conversation going:* Bring up a common interest shared by the two people or groups you're introducing: "Kyle and Suzie are thinking of redecorating their house. Aunt Jenny, you and Uncle Fred just redid yours last year, didn't you?" Then simply step back and watch the conversation take off.

  Once the conversation is kindled, discreetly slip away to greet the next guests: "I think someone's at the door. Excuse me, please . . ."

WHAT KIND OF PARTY DO YOU WANT TO THROW?

Every type of party has its own "feel"—the hum of voices at a dinner party where everyone is clicking, the chattering buzz of a happening cocktail party, the larger-than-life energy of a big bash with a friend spinning or a live band. The type of party you decide to give will depend on what kind of environment you want to create.

Cocktail Parties

To many people, "cocktail parties" bring to mind the not-so-swinging 1950s—yet here we are in the twenty-first century and we're still giving cocktail parties. *Cocktail party* is really a catchall term for any nondinner party you give where drinks and food are served. Cocktail parties can be large or small, fancy or casual, impromptu or planned for weeks. They may have elaborate hors d'oeuvres, or potato chips and takeout sushi. They're held to celebrate an engagement or an upcoming wedding; to honor a special guest, whether it's someone celebrating a birthday or the new guy on the block; or simply as an excuse to get people together.

For the newly independent, a cocktail party is a perfect introduction to entertaining, because it's a great opportunity to get people together for a fun evening of food and drinks without going to the time and trouble of serving a full-course meal.

Dinner Parties

Food is the ultimate social vehicle. Whenever people sit down together for a meal, there's an immediate sense of community and sharing. Whether you're hosting an intimate dinner for your best friends or putting on a lavish spread to impress your boss, you'll want your guests to

TEN GREAT DRINKS TO KNOW HOW TO MAKE WELL

When you're serving alcohol, it's always nice to have a roster of drinks that you can whip up on command. If you'd like to learn to make more than the ten cocktails listed here, *The Ultimate Bartender's Guide: 1000 Fabulous Recipes From the Four Seasons Restaurant* by Fred DuBose is an excellent, easy-to-read guide to making hundreds of great drinks.

1. *Bloody Mary:* 2 oz vodka, 3 oz tomato juice, 3 dashes Tabasco, 4 dashes clam juice, salt and pepper to taste; lime, celery, or a shelled clam for a garnish

2. *True Martini:* 3 oz vodka, 1 teaspoon dry vermouth; lemon twist or 3 olives for a garnish

3. *Cosmopolitan:* 2 oz vodka, 1 oz Cointreau, $1/2$ oz cranberry juice, $1/2$ oz fresh sour mix; lemon twist for garnish

4. *Mojito:* 1 teaspoon superfine sugar, 1 oz lime juice, 2 mint sprigs, 2 oz light rum, crushed ice, sparkling water; to get fancy, add a piece of sugar cane

5. *Gin Fizz:* $2^1/2$ oz gin, 1 oz sour mix, 4 oz club soda

6. *Perfect Manhattan:* $2^1/2$ oz rye whiskey, $1/4$ oz sweet & $1/4$ oz dry vermouth; lemon twist

7. *Bronx Tale:* 2 oz gin, 1 oz orange juice, 1 teaspoon dry vermouth

8. *Frozen Margarita:* In blender, combine 2 oz tequila, 1 oz Cointreau, 1 oz fresh sour mix, 1 splash Rose's Lime juice; mix with ice and turn on the blender*

9. *Four Seasons Hurricane:* 2 oz light rum, $1/2$ oz blue curaçao, $1/2$ oz pineapple juice, $1/2$ oz lemon juice, crushed ice, club soda; pineapple wedge for garnish

10. *Lizzie's Vodka Fizz:* 4 oz of your favorite vodka, club soda; lime

*Note: Before you offer to make anyone a margarita (or a piña colada, daiquiri, or other frozen drink), make sure your blender can actually crush ice.

~ TEN EASY HORS D'OEUVRES ~

- *Prosciutto-wrapped melon* or arugula
- *Bruschetta* (cut a baguette into slices, toast lightly, then top with a mixture of diced tomatoes, basil, garlic, and olive oil)
- *Shrimp cocktail*
- *Shrimp kabobs*
- *Chicken satay* (bite-sized pieces of boneless chicken, marinated and then broiled or grilled on a skewer and served with peanut sauce)
- *Nuts*
- *Smoked salmon on cucumber slices*
- *Chips and salsa with melted cheese on top* (leave a stack of small plates for people to serve themselves)
- *Cheese and crackers*
- *The mini-BLT* (make an ordinary BLT sandwich, then cut into quarters or smaller and secure each square with a toothpick)

leave feeling happy, sated, and wanting to come back. Dinner parties, like cocktail parties, run the gamut these days, from formal sit-down meals to informal buffets. It's really about your particular style of entertaining: If you're daring enough to plan and prepare an elaborate sit-down dinner party on your own, however, be careful to pin down exactly how many guests are coming!

To take the pressure off, many favor the potluck dinner party, where everyone is asked to bring a dish. Potlucks are fun, they're a great chance to try other people's food, they spread the work around, and they get everyone involved. As the host, it's your job to coordinate what everyone is bringing, so that everybody doesn't show up with a main course or dessert. (Also, remember to have some people bring the drinks—the noncooks in the group will usually be happy to do this.)

Whether you're hosting a six-course feast or a casual potluck dinner with friends, it's still up to you to treat your guests with hospitality and consideration. So dish out the food, refill the drinks, and let the good times roll!

Barbecues

Barbecues are my absolute favorite kinds of party to throw. Being outside in a pleasant setting with great food cooking away nearby is relaxing and totally entertaining. Throw in a bluegrass or classic rock CD, and what more could you ask for? Unlike a dinner party or cocktail party, where you're inviting your friends into your home, barbecues and other meals served outdoors are naturally relaxed affairs that provide a perfect breeding ground for enjoyable times. But don't forget: The barbecue may be outside, but people will still need to use your bathroom—so be sure to clean up your place before lighting the grill and opening your doors to guests (see the "Get-It-Together Party Prep List," page 77).

No-Fail Dinner #1: Shrimp Primavera

Shop for medium-size, uncooked shrimp (you'll need about 7 to 10 shrimp per person). Buy shrimp that already have split shells—this makes it easier to shell and de-vein them. Often you can pay a bit more to get them shelled and de-veined for you. But whatever you do, make sure you get uncooked shrimp.

    2 to 3 tablespoons olive oil
    3 cloves garlic
    1 medium onion, chopped
    1 medium red pepper, cut into long slivers
    1 handful spinach, washed and chopped
    2 handfuls fresh basil, rinsed and chopped
    Pasta; a little more than one handful per person (I like gemelli)

2 to 3 carrots, chopped
1 head of broccoli, washed and florets roughly chopped
1 pint half-and-half
2 teaspoons dried cilantro
1 teaspoon crushed black pepper
Freshly grated Parmesan cheese (roughly 1/2 to 1 cup)
Salt to taste

Fill a large pot with water for the pasta and set it to heat on high to boil. In a large saucepan over medium heat, heat 2 to 3 tablespoons of olive oil. Peel the garlic cloves and use the flat side of your knife to smush them, releasing the juices, then add the garlic to the olive oil in the pan. When the garlic is soft, remove it from the pan and set it aside. Next, add the chopped onions and the sliced bell pepper to the pan. Turn the heat down to medium low, and cook the onions and peppers, stirring occasionally, for 5 to 7 minutes or until limp. Add the spinach and one handful of basil to the peppers and onions. Chop two of the cloves of cooked garlic and add it to the rest of the vegetables, then continue cooking on low heat, stirring occasionally, as the spinach and basil wilt.

Add the pasta to the now-boiling water.

Place the carrots and broccoli florets in a microwave-safe bowl. Add a little water (1/4 cup or so), cover, and cook in the microwave for 3 to 4 minutes, then set aside until the dish is almost ready. (If the vegetables are undercooked, keep popping them into the microwave for 1-minute increments until done.)

Now for the sauce: In a medium saucepan, heat a pint of half-and-half over medium-low heat. Mince the remaining clove of cooked garlic and add to the sauce. Add the cilantro, black pepper, and remaining basil, and salt to taste. Continue cooking on medium-low heat. As the sauce heats, add the freshly grated Parmesan cheese and stir with a whisk. (The cheese will help thicken the sauce.) Watch your sauce carefully, making sure it doesn't start to boil.

When the pasta is done, drain it and set it aside. Add the shrimp to the pan, and sprinkle a little salt over the vegetables and shrimp. Cook the shrimp quickly for 3 to 4 minutes (they're done when they curl up and turn pink). Add the sauce and pasta to the veggies and shrimp. This dish tastes terrific topped with grated Parmesan.

P.S.: Need a great vegetarian dish? Ditch the shrimp and you've got one!

No-Fail Dinner #2: The Best Kabob Recipe Ever

This recipe is killer and it works on everything: chicken, shrimp, beef, or pork. It's a no-fail dish—in fact, you barely need measuring cups to make it.

Meat of choice, cut into bite-sized chunks (or medium-sized shrimp)
$1/2$ onion, grated
$1/2$ cup olive oil
Juice from $1/2$ to 1 whole lemon
2 to 3 tablespoons curry powder
1 teaspoon ground coriander
1 teaspoon ground ginger
1 clove of garlic, mashed to a pulp
2 teaspoons of crushed chili peppers or red pepper flakes (all to taste, mind you)

Combine the ingredients in a bowl, then add your meat of choice (my personal favorites are shrimp and pork tenderloin), and refrigerate for at least 30 minutes. Next, spear the meat onto a barbecue stick and throw it on the grill.

P.S.: This dish is especially great when the meat is alternated on the stick with chunks of grilled onion, bell pepper, and pineapple. (Don't place the pineapple directly next to the chicken, as it causes the chicken to go soft.)

~~ INSTANT TIP ~~~~~~~~~~~~~~~~~~~~~~~~~~~

W hen making kabobs, soak the wooden skewers in warm water for about ten minutes before spearing the veggies and meat on. This will keep them from burning and breaking on the grill.

Wine-Tasting Parties

In an effort to better educate themselves about wine, some friends of mine have starting hosting wine-tasting parties. They're not alone; wine-tasting parties are popping up practically everywhere these days, in big cities and small towns and in every age group. How it works: The guests choose a few bottles of wine, and then prepare light hors d'oeuvres to pair with them. Guests typically number from eight to fifteen people, and each should bring a bottle or two of wine to taste. Often the host determines the types of wine for the evening's tasting (full-bodied reds, for example, or dessert wines) and then pairs the nibbles accordingly. A wine tasting is a great way to have a light night of socializing, learn a bit about wine, and get together with friends.

Possible themes for a wine-tasting party include:

- Same wine, different years
- All reds, all whites, or all blushes
- All wines from a certain region
- The same kind of wine from different regions

"Party" Parties: Big, Small, and in Between

Big bashes can be a blast. They're a great way to get a ton of people together, and they're always memorable events. When hosting a large

HEADS UP: GOT GLASSES?

[W]hen hosting a wine tasting, you'll need to make sure you have enough wine glasses to serve all of your guests both white and red wine. Here is what a white-wine glass (left) and a red-wine glass (right) look like.

party, however, in addition to following the Get-It-Together Party Prep List (see page 77), take the precaution of putting away anything especially fragile or expensive—your favorite painting, that pricey crystal vase, the box where you keep your jewelry, even your DVD collection—so it doesn't get stolen or broken. That's the catch with big parties: Because they aren't small, friends of friends usually show up, and sometimes even passersby find their way in. This can be exciting—you never know *who* will show up for a big party—but it also means you need to be ready for the unexpected.

This sort of party probably isn't that far removed from the big parties you attended when you were younger—but if you're like a lot of newly independents, you may find that you prefer a slightly smaller version as you get (dare I say it) older. Midsize-to-small parties are much more manageable than large, kegger-style deals, and they create a certain feeling of togetherness that ragers lack—which is why they're often more suitable for celebrations such as birthdays, going-away par-

I f you're throwing a big party, let your neighbors know ahead of time. Then double-check to make *sure* that they know, and that they have your phone number, in case your party gets too loud. Believe me, this is in your best interest; because if they *don't* have your number, I can guarantee they have the number for the police—and noise violation fines can be very expensive.

ties, and promotions. (Not to say that a huge party isn't fun for these celebrations as well!)

Smaller parties also hold different responsibilities for the host than do big parties. Cleaning up the strewn CDs, beer cans, and spilled food after a major bash can be overwhelming—as can worrying about possible damage to your place, which you could be financially responsible for. Sometimes it's easier to concern yourself with simply making sure the beer cooler is full, throwing on some tunes, and having a great time with friends you know, love, and trust. And therein lies the wonderful intimacy of a small party: You as the host get to spend time with the people you want to spend time with.

So, whether you're hosting the party event of the year or you and your closest friends are meeting over a pizza to watch the Yankees and Red Sox duke it out one more time, always keep in mind the one basic secret of entertaining and bringing friends together: It's about ensuring that a good time is had by all.

CHICKFEST

C hristina's sister Nifer and her roommates used to throw a "ChickFest" party every couple of months, each of them inviting a handful of girls they knew and liked. Everyone would bring a dish, and Nifer and her roommates would make party favors like white mugs decorated with the words *Chick Fest* and little cartoons drawn in colored permanent markers and then fill them with knickknacks. The idea was simple, really: just a chance for a bunch of girls to eat some good grub, drink wine, and enjoy one another's company, and, well, just be chicks.

THE UNOFFICIAL RULES OF BEER PONG

As long as we're discussing big parties, it seems appropriate to pay homage to a game I once loved: beer pong. Since every crowd has its own specific version, what follows are just the basics; feel free to tweak them as you see fit.

All you need is a table—most often created out of a door taken from its hinges and placed over two desk chairs, though it can also be a Ping-Pong table, a folding table, or whatever, just so it's long and waist-high—some plastic cups, and lots of beer. Here's how to play the 10-cup version of the game: At either end of the table, each two-player team places ten cups in the shape of a pyramid. The point of your team's pyramid should be farthest away from you and the four base cups should aligned along the edge of the table closest to you.

Fill each cup with two to three inches of beer, then fill two extra cups with water for rinsing beer off the Ping-Pong balls. (They'll need it.) The team that starts gets two Ping-Pong balls, one for each player.

The idea is to toss your ball into one of the opposing team's cups. When you do this, one of your opponents has to drink the cup of beer that the ball landed in.

- Re-racking takes place when you eliminate enough of your opponent's cups to create a smaller pyramid.

- When there are just two cups left, the team throwing can request that they be lined up one right in front of the other.

- When both teammates land a ball in a cup, they receive another turn.

- If a ball does not go directly into the beer but instead swirls around the rim of the cup, one defender (usually a girl) can attempt to blow the ball out of the cup.

- If both players shoot at the same time and their Ping-Pong balls land in the same cup, they win outright. Otherwise, the team that eliminates the other team's cups first is the winner.

DRINKING AND DRIVING

Parties are great. And being young and independent at them is even greater. But because alcohol is so very much a part of our party culture, it's important to remember that as the host you are legally responsible for anything that happens to the guests you provided with alcohol for as long as that alcohol is in their system. If someone leaves your home and gets into a car accident, or even is injured in a fight, you could find yourself in court. When guests have clearly had too much to drink, preventing them from driving away and calling for a cab to take them home instead isn't just the right thing to do—it's your legal obligation.

WHEN *YOU'RE* THE GUEST . . .

Offer to help out.

Be a conversationalist (see "Dinner Conversation," page 151).

Don't overstay your welcome.

Don't snoop.

Offer to bring something . . .

- To an informal party, bring some chips and salsa or cheese and crackers or maybe a dessert.
- To a formal party, a bottle of wine or a box of chocolates makes a great offering.

- When the last cup is eliminated, the losing team is allowed one rebuttal turn or two last shots.

- The losing team has to finish the winning team's beer.

- The winning team stays on the table to challenge the next team up.

KNOWING WHEN IT'S TIME TO GO

The party was one of the best you've ever thrown. Most of the people have left, but a small group of people has lingered on, talking until well past midnight. Still, all good things must come to an end, and now it's time to pull the plug so you can crawl into bed. How to let your guests know that the party's over—without actually kicking them out?

Basically, there are four levels of signals that a host can send (and that guests should be looking for):

1. You say something like, "Well it's been a wonderful evening, but unfortunately I have to get up early tomorrow . . ."

2. If that doesn't work, begin gathering up the plates, cups, and napkins; wiping down the tables; and doing the dishes. Once you start cleaning up, most people will realize it's time to say their good-byes and go. Your guests can take the hint then and there or, better yet, pitch in and help in the cleaning before bowing out the door.

3. If you finish cleaning up and your guests are still hanging around, a comment like, "Well, folks, I think it's time to call it a night" should get through to even the most obtuse guest.

4. Finally, if all else fails, simply usher your guests to the door and say, "Thanks for coming. Good night!" as you gently propel them over the threshold.

PART 2

THE REST OF THE WORLD AND YOU

CHAPTER 8

STEPPIN' OUT:

WHAT YOU'RE TELLING THE WORLD

OW MANY TIMES have you and your friends been walking along and seen some girl in a miniskirt suctioned to her butt, wearing bulky high heels and a top that makes you wonder *Real or fake?* Someone says, "Oh my God, can you believe what she's wearing?" Or maybe no one says it, but you all think it. The point is, the way she dresses affects your impression of her. Chances are, she's a totally normal, nice person, and had no intention whatsoever of looking so provocative. But because of her clothing, you can't help but judge her differently.

The fact of the matter is, *appearance matters.* How we dress, smell, speak, and use our body language and even things like smoking will all affect the way the outside world sees us. While there will always be those who disagree with your sense of style or your personal life choices, one thing that you do have complete control over is how much influence your lifestyle has on your outward appearance.

I wish we lived in a world where appearances didn't matter. But the truth is, we don't. And since appearances *do* matter, it's much better to try and use appearance to our advantage rather than let it get the better of us. Ultimately, of course, you'll have to use your own best judgment when you decide how much you're going to clean yourself up before stepping out. There are definitely days when I'll get up, skip my shower, throw on my comfy jeans (as opposed to my supercute, going-out jeans), throw my hair up in a messy bun or ponytail, grab a piece of gum, and walk downtown for a cup of coffee. If I'm meeting a friend for coffee, I'll put a little more effort into my appearance. Maybe I'll wash my face and apply some makeup. And if we're going to a nicer place for coffee—or if we're headed to brunch—I'll take a shower and make sure my outfit is clean and cute.

Whatever you decide, make sure you're comfortable and clean when you step outside your door. And don't forget that surprises can (and will) happen. I've never forgotten the day I bumped into a crush of mine on my way to get coffee after a *very* late night out. Beyond checking the mirror to make sure I was still a member of the living, I had put no effort whatsoever into cleaning myself up. When I saw the guy in question, my hand automatically flew up to my hair to see if it was greasy or knotted or what. *I wish I'd run a comb through it!* I thought with sudden chagrin. When he turned and spotted me looking the way I did, I cringed.

So no, you're not being neurotic when you put in a little extra grooming before stepping out, even if it's just to get the paper. *You're making yourself comfortable and giving yourself the confidence to deal with anything the world is going to throw you.* Trust me—it'll save you from cringing the way I did.

HOW WE DRESS

Anyone who's gone people-watching knows that our wardrobe sends strong signals about who we are and what we're doing. A T-shirt, torn jeans, and flip-flops say one thing: *I'm out, probably not meeting a date, just minding my own business, maybe running a quick errand.* Khakis, a polo shirt, and sandals say another: *I could be on my way to lunch with someone I like, or I like to look a little sharper when I walk out my door.*

Don't get me wrong—I've frequently been known to model my painting jeans, tank top, and a button-down worn loosely with a pair of slide-on sandals. The point is, *how* you choose to dress makes a statement. So doesn't it make sense to take a moment and think about exactly what kind of statement you want to make? The key is to let your choice of wardrobe be guided by whatever situations you plan to be in, then take another second to think about what situations might crop up that you *haven't* planned on (like bumping into someone you're interested in).

Dressing Day to Day

When you're just kicking around—doing errands, hanging out with friends, or whatever—dude, wear what you want, but be aware that your fashion choices send messages and that you don't want that message misinterpreted. There are times when our appearance doesn't make much difference to those around us—for instance, with people we pass on the street. You can wear the craziest outfit and it won't affect a bunch of strangers in the slightest. The same goes for what *they're* wearing: If it's weird, who cares? But what if you should happen to run into your boss on the street and you're wearing fishnets under Daisy Dukes and a ripped-to-shreds, off-the-shoulder T-shirt? You still might not care—but what if your boss does? Or what if you spot your boss's uncomfortable reaction to your wardrobe and end up feeling embarrassed yourself?

The chances of this kind of awkward encounter can be avoided completely with a little planning. Whenever you're dressing, even if it's just everyday wear, consider what message your outfit will display to different people you might encounter. Feel prepared and confident to run into pals, work acquaintances, shop employees, even potential dates when you're steppin' out.

Getting Ready for Steppin' Out

There's a reason why we dress up for dates, parties, openings, meetings, and other get-togethers. At all of these events, we are literally dressing to impress others. This means not simply wearing an outfit that will turn heads (not that there's anything wrong with that!), but also choosing a wardrobe that is tasteful, stylish, and appropriate to the event—one that shows your respect for the occasion. Different occasions, naturally, call for different styles. Every event offers a unique opportunity to say what you want to about yourself and to make a favorable impression on old friends and new acquaintances alike.

Dressing for a Date

Whether you're on a first date, heading out on the town with your boyfriend or girlfriend, or celebrating a special anniversary, dates are a time to dress up a notch for an intimate time together—so make the most of the opportunity.

Clothing

There are times when what you wear can really set the tone for the evening. Dressing up for someone else is a way of showing them that your shared time together is important enough to spend some extra time on looking nice. (For more specifics, see box, "Dressing Up for Dining Out," page 144.)

Case in point: My friend Lyndsay had been dating her boyfriend for a year. To celebrate, she decided to take him out to dinner at a nice restaurant. She made the reservation, and the two of us went shopping to dress her up. She was really excited about the night: She borrowed some jewelry and spent a considerable amount of time getting ready over at my place. When her boyfriend arrived to pick her up, she looked fantastic. Unfortunately, her boyfriend didn't. Jeans and an old T-shirt would have been fine for an everyday hangout, but for an anniversary dinner at a nice restaurant, the outfit just didn't cut it. Lyndsay was really disappointed. She had wanted a special evening, and he had given her everyday casual.

Appearance

When going out on a date, your appearance should be as welcoming as what you wear. Besides being clean (shower fresh), you should look clean and feel comfortable in what you're wearing. I'll never forget once seeing a woman out on a date wearing a slightly off-the-shoulder

THE DAY THE POSTS WERE ASKED TO LEAVE THE RITZ

When I was about twelve, my dad, my sister, and I went to New York City for the weekend to see a hockey game. My dad thought it would be fun to take his country bumpkins out to brunch someplace nice, and so we headed to the Ritz. The Ritz, as it turned out, had a no-jeans policy. So when my sister walked in with her very clean, wrinkle-free jeans and a nice button-down shirt, we were told very kindly that we could not be served. We wound up having a great brunch at the Four Seasons instead. It goes to show, however, that when places have set rules, they tend to abide by them. If you are told that you don't meet the dress code, don't be offended, and *definitely* don't try to argue: Just realize that today isn't the day to eat at that particular restaurant, thank the staff politely, and leave.

top that kept slipping down her arms. She spent the majority of the evening trying to keep her top up. *Not* comfortable.

Fragrance

In an effort to seem mature, maybe even cool, the middle-school boys who I student-taught would load on cologne and body spray by the gallon. I can only hope that by the time they get to be our age, they'll understand the less-is-more theory of perfumes and other scents.

One problem is that people often use fragrance to cover up bad odors. All that does, however, is add good odor to bad—it doesn't take the bad smell away. The idea in wearing fragrance is first to get clean, and then give yourself a fresher scent.

Even if you've come straight out of the shower, it's easy to spritz on too much perfume or cologne. With any scent, the secret is to apply just the right amount. Here's what to do: Spray two to three squirts into the air, and then *walk through the mist you've created.* Then put the bottle down: you're done. Guys can try this trick: Put a small drop of cologne in the palm of your hand, then rub your hands together and pat your cheeks (the ones on your face, that is).

Dressing for Parties

This is one issue that has sent countless party-goers into fits of indecision—as any guy who's waited for his date to choose an outfit knows. While picking out the perfect thing to wear is never easy, finding out the appropriate *type* of attire is: Just pick up the phone, call your hosts, and ask what people will be wearing.

At a Formal Evening Event

If you are attending a formal evening event, you *really* need to make sure that you're dressed appropriately. Short dresses, wrinkled shirts, or any items that are too tight or too loose make you stick out like a sore thumb—and on a night like this, that's *not* how you want to make heads turn. When you get an invitation to a formal evening event, think sophisticated and classy. This doesn't have to mean boring, however—the fashion industry has proved that formal evening attire can be beautiful, bold, and *very* eye-catching, not to mention a great conversation starter. Just make sure you're eye-catching for the right reasons.

Women should wear long dresses or knee-length cocktail dresses. Skirt-and-top combinations are acceptable as well, but the skirt shouldn't be too far above your knees and the combination should be elegant, rather than businesslike or as if you've dressed for a night out with your friends. As far as showing skin is concerned, it's really up to you—the only question is, are you going to be comfortable with the amount of attention you draw to yourself? Open-backed, spaghetti-strap, halter, or sleeveless styles are all fine, as long as you feel comfortable and confident in what you're wearing.

A TUX TO CALL YOUR OWN

I f you're a guy and you plan to be attending any black-tie events in the near future, the easiest thing is to have your own tux hanging in your closet, ready to go. Renting a tux is easy, too, of course. But here's a tip: The next time you go into the rental shop, once you've picked out a tux you like, ask the store manager how much it would cost simply to buy the tux instead of renting it. When my father did this, he found (as will you) that the purchase price was very reasonable—the equivalent of just three rentals. So, to save himself money and hassle, he went ahead and bought the tuxedo. After he bought a tux shirt to go with it, he was set for any formal event for the next ten years. Easy and cost effective—you've gotta love it.

INSTANT TIP

I f you're ever unsure about wearing a certain outfit to an event, consult a friend or coworker who might be going, or call the establishment where the event is being held.

Men should wear coats and ties, along with dress shoes. Clothing should be clean and wrinkle-free, and shoes should be polished. If the invitation indicates that black tie is either required or preferred, you'll really need a tuxedo. And don't feel embarrassed or overdressed when you wear it: If any of those words are on the invitation, you can be assured that other men will be wearing tuxes as well. In fact, if tuxes are required, you'll find yourself feeling very out of place if you wear a suit. If the invitation says "black tie optional," then a suit will do—but a tux would still be a sharp choice.

HOW WE EXPRESS OURSELVES

When it comes to how we speak, it's really a Goldilocks situation: The language we use has to be just right in order for us to be understood. The actual act of talking is incredibly complex, when you think about it. Voice inflection, tone, speed, volume, vocabulary, and body movements are all used to help us communicate with each other. The words we use, and how we choose to use them, literally speak volumes about who we are. Language reflects how we think and feel—and in doing so, it can be friend or foe.

Look at it this way: If you were being interviewed for a magazine article, you'd want the writer to quote you correctly, right? The same holds true when you're crafting a presentation, asking someone out on

~ ETIQUETTE AT A GLANCE ~

WHAT TO WEAR WHEN

Whatever type of event you plan on attending, you'll always be safe if you follow one simple guideline: When in doubt, err on the formal side. The more elaborate the occasion, the more true this is. Formal or semiformal events aren't a time to take risks. Remember, confidence shows—so if you're unsure of what you're wearing, choose something else that you are sure of. When you wear clothes that you feel comfortable and confident in, your focus will be on the evening and not on your outfit.

MEN	WOMEN
White Tie	
• Black tailcoat, matching trousers with a single stripe of satin or braid	• Formal (floor-length) evening gown
• White piqué wing-collared shirt with stiff front	
• White vest	
• White bow tie	
• White or gray gloves	
• Black patent-leather shoes and black dress socks	

MEN	WOMEN
Black Tie	
• Black tuxedo jacket and matching trousers	• Formal (floor-length) evening gown or short, dressy cocktail dress
• Formal (piqué or pleated front) white shirt	

CONTINUED

MEN	WOMEN
• Black bow tie (silk, shiny satin, or twill) • Black cummerbund to match tie • Dressy suspenders to ensure a good fit (optional) • Black patent-leather shoes and black dress socks • No gloves • *In summer or on a cruise:* white dinner jacket; black tuxedo trousers plus other black-tie wardrobe	• Formal (floor-length) evening gown or short, dressy cocktail dress

MEN	WOMEN

Black Tie Optional

MEN	WOMEN
• Either a tuxedo (see "Black Tie" above) *or* • Dark suit, white shirt, and conservative tie	• Formal (floor-length) evening gown *or* • Short, dressy cocktail dress or dressy separates

MEN	WOMEN

Creative Black Tie

MEN	WOMEN
• Tuxedo combined with trendy or whimsical items, such as a black shirt or a matching colored or patterned bow tie and cummerbund • Black shiny patent-leather or dressy black leather shoes and black socks	• Formal (floor-length) evening gown, *or* • Short, dressy cocktail dress or dressy separates *or* • Any of the above accessorized with such items as a feather boa, colorful shawl, or colorful jewelry

CONTINUED

MEN	WOMEN

Semiformal

MEN	WOMEN
• Dark business suit (usually worsted wool)	• Short afternoon or cocktail dress, or long, dressy skirt and top
• Matching vest (optional)	
• White shirt	
• Conservative tie	
• Dressy leather shoes and dress (dark) socks	

MEN	WOMEN

Festive Attire

MEN	WOMEN
• Seasonal sport coat or blazer in color of choice and slacks, *with*	• Short cocktail dress *or*
• Open-collar shirt *or*	• Long, dressy skirt and top *or*
• Shirt and "festive" or holiday-themed tie	• Dressy pants outfit

MEN	WOMEN

Dressy Casual

MEN	WOMEN
• Seasonal sport coat or blazer and slacks	• Street-length dress *or*
• Open-collar shirt	• Skirt and dressy top *or*
	• Dressy pants outfit

MEN	WOMEN

Business Casual

MEN	WOMEN
• Seasonal sport coat or blazer with slacks or khakis	• Skirt, khakis, or slacks

CONTINUED

MEN	WOMEN
• Open-collar shirt	• Open-collar shirt, knit shirt, or sweater (no spaghetti straps or décolleté)

MEN	WOMEN

Sport Casual

MEN	WOMEN
• Khakis or clean, pressed jeans	• Khakis or clean, pressed jeans
• Plain T-shirt (no slogans), polo shirt, *or*	• Plain T-shirt (no slogans), polo shirt, *or*
• Casual button-down shirt	• Casual button-down shirt

MEN	WOMEN

Beach Casual

MEN	WOMEN
• Khakis or shorts (cargo or Bermuda)	• Sundress, khakis, or shorts (cargo or Bermuda)
• Knit or polo shirt	• Open-collar, knit, or polo shirt
• Sport jacket (optional) or sweater	• Lightweight jacket or sweater

MEN	WOMEN

Holiday Casual

MEN	WOMEN
• Clothing is the same as for "Business Casual" with some holiday colors or designs	• Clothing is the same as for "Business Casual" with some holiday colors or designs

a date, or introducing a band. You want to get your message across clearly—you want your audience to be informed and impressed, or the girl or guy to say yes or the crowd to go wild.

That's why, when we're speaking with someone outside our circle of best friends and family—those who know us very well—it's important to choose our words, tones, and inflections more carefully. When I started my semester of student teaching, my cooperating teacher took me aside and told me that some of the students were a little intimidated by me because I have such a theatrical vocal style. When I'd call to get their attention (and in a busy art room, that's not an easy thing to get) I would literally shout, "Yo, everybody listen up!"—and then continue speaking in a loud voice once my students had settled down.

"Not only are you intimidating the kids," my cooperating teacher said, "but it's wearing out your voice." She suggested that I use my "booming" voice to get the students' attention, wait for a minute for everyone to settle down, and then resume in a normal speaking voice. I realized that I'd thought I needed that loud voice for teaching, but I didn't. Once I softened my tone and volume, the kids started responding much more positively to me. Little did I realize it, but they had thought I was angry at them! Once I added the pause and volume control, they understood that my "loud" voice just meant that I had an announcement to make. Simply altering the volume of my voice changed how the kids interpreted what I was saying—which changed everything.

TO SWEAR OR NOT TO SWEAR?

I'm not going to say that swearing or telling dirty jokes or using other off-color language is taboo or wrong. Obviously, it finds its way into my vocabulary on occasion. In fact, there is some bizarre attraction to swearing, and even a certain sense of independence around the fact

YOUR SISTER HAS A MOUTH LIKE A TRUCKER

fter my freshman year at college, I wanted out of the dorms. I asked my parents if they would let me move off-campus. They said no. There was a lot more to this conversation, actually, but that's essentially what it boiled down to. So I called my sister to vent about the situation. I got her answering machine, and all my pent-up frustration came pouring out in my message.

My sister's roommate came home to the machine later that evening and heard:

"You have two new messages. Message number one, four forty-two PM. *'I can't believe it! Don't Mom and Dad know how f***ing awful the dorms are. I mean f***! It's so sh***y here, Anna; I hate it so much. I can't f***ing do my artwork. For f***'s sake, why can't they . . . I mean, my God, how the hell am I supposed to get any work done? This is f***ing ridicu—'* " Beep. "Message number two, four forty-six PM . . . *'I mean, how am I supposed to f***ing handle this? I can't concentrate worth sh**. . . . Mom and Dad are only doing this to get that last god**** stranglehold on me . . . Ergg!'* "

Anna came home a little later. "You got a message from your sister today," her roommate said. "Boy, she has a mouth like a trucker!"

Cringe.

Guilty as charged. I *did* have "a mouth like a trucker." When Anna told me about this, we both laughed—but I knew I had gone too far with my message. I apologized to her and her roommate. I still haven't met the roommate, but I can only imagine what he thinks of me.

---

that we can now do it without a parent there to correct us with, "That *darn* car . . ." Swearing is a part of our language at certain times in life. And there's no denying that when carefully chosen, curse words can give statements a certain emphasis that other words can't match.

What you want to watch out for, however, is *who* you're swearing in front of. If you're on the street and a group of young children pass by, for example, are you going to let the "f" word slip, or are you going to hold it back? When you go to visit your girlfriend's parents, will you be swearing a blue streak? When you're talking with people at the water cooler, what kind of self-censorship will you practice, even if your colleagues aren't using any?

During my student-teaching experience I learned that swearing in a school is disastrous—especially if any kids hear you. I quickly had to learn to curb my tongue. Two weeks of swearing detox, in which I tried not to allow a single blue word to cross my lips, took me from newly independent college mode (using swear words simply because I could) to newly independent professional mode (no swearing). It worked—I think.

THE 3 A'S:
ATTITUDES, ACTIONS,
AND ASSUMPTIONS

Wherever you happen to be and whomever you happen to run into, it's always important to consider your attitudes and actions, and what assumptions they may be encouraging other people to make about you.

While it's true that, as the saying goes, to assume can sometimes make an "ass" out of "u" and "me," in reality, *assumptions* are what we base many of our interactions on. We form these assumptions about other people from their *actions*—literally what they do—and their *attitudes*—the emotional output that goes with their actions. When my class heard my booming voice (an action of mine, albeit unintentional), they assumed I was angry at them.

One issue that research for this book revealed was that people sometimes have a problem with being *too* nice. They find that if they're polite and friendly to an acquaintance at a bar, or to a friend of a friend, or to a coworker, or to someone else they really aren't interested in hanging out with, suddenly they'll get deluged with phone calls inviting them on dates—and, worse still, they don't know how to refuse the invitations.

When your actions and attitudes are friendly, even if you think you're "faking it," other people are going to assume that you enjoy their company. So, what should you do when you encounter those people who you don't want to make a part of your social circle but who are still good people?

Respect them. Respect them for who they are as individuals. Remember that you can still abide by the principles of etiquette—consideration, respect, and honesty—without actually liking someone. You might be honest, considerate, and respectful toward your boss, but that doesn't mean you want to socialize with him. Or maybe you have a family member whom you love but with whom you don't like to hang out.

The key is to look past the obnoxious voice or the annoying mannerisms; then we can begin to listen to the person we are with rather than just contemplating whether or not we like him or her. This is true of anyone we listen to: professor, boss, parent, friend. All have qualities that we choose to ignore so that we can focus on the content of what they're saying. This is where respect comes in. When you interact with someone in a respectful and considerate way, personal idiosyncrasies are forgotten, leaving you to enjoy the conversation.

On the other hand, what if it's the content of the conversation that's driving you nuts? Suppose another person has a habit of making bigoted remarks or is always bringing up issues that you feel are inappropriate? (See "Instant Tip," page 118.) Or maybe you just feel like you have nothing to contribute to the conversation or that you're a third wheel. I once spent a weekend at the house of a friend. She had moved

SAYING NO FOR THE RIGHT REASONS

 ooner or later, you're going to hear someone you don't know well—maybe they're an old school acquaintance or a friend of a friend—asking if you'd like to hang out, go on a date, meet for dinner, whatever. What do you do if you don't want to say yes? It's not that you don't like this person, but you barely have enough time for the friends and responsibilities you have now. Solution—tell the truth, as nicely as you can: "I'm sorry, but right now my life is incredibly hectic, and my schedule is packed. Why don't you give me your number? Maybe we can get together sometime when things calm down."

---

recently, and she invited her only friend in her new town to come over. All the friend did was talk about work and her boyfriend and other friends whom I knew nothing about. She was completely oblivious of the fact that her conversation was all about things I couldn't comment on. *I'm in someone else's life right now, not mine,* I thought. So I listened, and I gave input where I could. Having previously lived with the girl I was visiting, I could tell that it was driving her nuts. Finally, my host said with a smile, "I'm sure you'll figure it out [meaning her and the boyfriend, etc.]. However, we do need to talk about what we're doing tonight . . ." and I was saved.

Still, there will be times when you find you're the odd man out on an issue, and you may feel pressured to talk about stuff you don't want to. One of the people interviewed for this book reported that though he was happy at his new job, he was having a hard time fitting in because conversations at the office were often about other coworkers or company politics. He finally decided he simply wasn't going to look for any work friends among the people who gossiped. I thought that was a really smart move.

INSTANT TIP

emember: The principles of etiquette give you the tools to control any situation. If you aren't comfortable with the way a certain conversation is going, *politely say to the other person, "I'm sorry, I'm just not comfortable with this conversation."* Or simply refuse to engage yourself in the conversation, and quietly leave.

THE LITTLE STUFF

Don't you wish that people were always nice and thoughtful? We live in a fast-paced, stressful world, where people don't always consider the effects of their actions on others. The snide comments, the change being tossed at you across the counter, the honking when you find yourself in the wrong lane—I don't know about you, but it makes me depressed to think about how inconsiderate the world has gotten at times.

You know how it is when you're having a bad day, and then someone does something kind such as running after you with something you dropped, or noticing that your pants are ripped or stained in a place you wouldn't have seen? They just do or say some nice thing, and it's like a breath of fresh air that recharges you and gives you a little more hope for the day. That's the power of simple acts of etiquette to change our world.

A pharmacy clerk rang up my purchase one day. After she tossed the change on the counter, I asked her if she could give me two five-dollar bills in exchange for my ten. She looked at me as if I'd asked her to go clean my toilet. She shoved the change into my hand and then stood there glaring for what seemed like a minute. "What do you want, a bag?" she said finally.

"Yes, I really would," I said. "Thank you." She slowly dropped the items in, one by one, and then handed me the bag. All I could think was, *Damn, this girl has attitude!* As I left, I looked her straight in the eye and sincerely said to her, "Have a nice day."

Yes, she had a crappy attitude. Yes, I thought she was totally rude. Yes, I could have asked to speak to her manager and gotten her yelled at for providing poor customer service. And yes, I've had bad days, too, when I fervently wished for that one nice person to come along. (For more on the etiquette of shopping, see Chapter 9, "Errands," page 120.)

Thinking about this incident afterward, I was struck by the realization that if I made a conscious effort to act with more consideration and understanding, maybe I could become one more of those nice people we run into during the day—and maybe this attitude would even spread to someone else in the process.

Your appearance, what you say, and how you carry yourself *matter* whenever you're stepping out of your home. Remember: *You* are the one who controls the impression the world has of you.

CHAPTER 9

ERRANDS

O NE OF THE MAIN ISSUES we face as young independents is being taken seriously by the world around us. It's all too easy, especially for those of us in school, to get lumped under the dreaded label "college kids." I was reading a magazine article the other day about the best breakfast places in town for under $5. The writer gave five stars to a slightly out-of-the-way diner because the food and selection for the price were great—and then went on to add that since it's a bit more of a local place, you won't run into as many "pajama-wearing college kids" gabbing about party drama and procrastination. *Ouch.*

Now that we're on our own, all we want is a little respect, right? When it comes to running errands, that means being treated as a bona fide customer, on the same level as everyone else. If you've ever had a job selling retail goods or serving food, I'm sure you remember trying to avoid certain shoppers after seeing or overhearing them, thinking to yourself, *Oh please, I don't have the energy for this today.* The customers who were polite, on the other hand, were the ones you tried to help out.

The best way to get good service is simply to be a good customer.

But when you're caught up in the weekly five-mile dash—grocery store, pharmacy, returning that item of clothing, a quick stop at a friend's place, then back out to the store for a new DVD before grabbing something quick to eat—it's easy to forget how to be that good customer. Errands, it seems, always have to be done when you're already late for something really important—such as work, or class, a date, or some well-deserved "chill time." It's so easy to get annoyed and tap your foot impatiently or even huff out loud (while griping silently to yourself) over the fact that you have only one item and the person ahead of you with the overflowing shopping cart didn't let you go ahead.

Want to know what's worse? Being the cashier who has to put up with your impatience.

Now, I'm not always an angel when it comes to errands myself. But errands are a part of life. As important as *my* life may be to me, this clerk I'm tapping my foot at has a life, too, and she deserves all the respect I can give her. My point here is that we *all* have busy schedules, with places to go and people to meet. There's no reason why we have to make someone else's life unpleasant just because we happen to be pressed for time while they're at work.

ERRAND ETIQUETTE

"Errand etiquette" begins as soon as you enter a store, and continues until you walk out the door:

The Entrance

It's simple and so nice to acknowledge the staff of the place where you're shopping. If someone greets you when you first enter a store, be sure to respond. All you have to do is smile and say hi in return. If they don't greet you? Say hi anyway. Often you'll get a look of surprise, and then a smile and a greeting in response. Nice, huh?

Once You're In

Now you're in, hunting through the store trying to get what you need and get out. The mission is on. The only problem: you can't find one of the items that you're looking for. *Great*, you mutter to yourself. Then you spot a person with a name tag and make a beeline for him. But wait—coming from the opposite direction, some lady snags your potential time-saver. *Ergg!* You keep moving, trying desperately to locate your item without being distracted by other, more enticing goods. Finally you spot another clerk and approach her warily, glancing around as you do. Good—you're the only customer in sight.

Asking for Help

In some stores, the salespeople would be all over you offering assistance. Here, they're nowhere to be seen—and when you do track someone down, she doesn't seem to have the slightest idea where anything is. What do you do? Yes, you're rushed. Yes, you're frustrated. No, you don't act impatient. Now is an excellent time to remind yourself that this per-

INSTANT TIP

When you're finished trying on clothes in a store's fitting room, don't leave the clothing in a heap on the floor. Instead, put the clothes back on the hangers. Then, depending on the store's policy, leave them inside or just outside the dressing room, or place them back on the sales racks.

son is going to *try* help you—and if she can't (maybe the item is out of stock or in a different department, or maybe she's new on the job and has to refer you to another salesperson), that's okay, too. Have patience, and remember that any aggression you're feeling stems from the unfound item, not the clerk's actions.

Keep in mind, too, that it's unfair to ask any salesperson to break the rules for you, even if she's a friend. A cup of coffee costs $2, only three items can be taken into a fitting room at a time—whatever the rule is, when you ask someone to make an exception for you, you're essentially asking them to risk their job.

When you approach a salesperson, there are three phrases that are guaranteed to help you get the assistance you need:

- **Excuse me.** Saying *excuse me* signals to the person you're approaching that you understand she's currently in the middle of doing something else, even if she's just walking down the store aisle. For all you know, that salesperson could be headed to take a break, or make an important phone call, or punch out for the day. Saying excuse me shows you are considerate of the fact that she may be busy, regardless of how things may appear.

- **Please.** *Please* really is a magic word. I'm not joking. By saying *please,* you let the other person know that you are neither expecting nor demanding their help but instead are nicely requesting it. The tone created by the word *please* is one of polite inquiry. Think about it—which do you respond better to: "Where's the milk?" or, "Where's the milk, please?" If you're still not convinced, tune in to your inner monologue the next time someone *doesn't* say *please* to you, and see if you hear grumbling inside your head.

- **Thank you.** *Thank you* is absolutely key. The job of people in service and sales positions is to help you, the customer. So,

THE RIGHT RESPONSE TO RUDE BEHAVIOR

No matter how rude other people may be, it's not our job to make their manners better or to fail to give them good service just because they're being inconsiderate. Two wrongs don't make a right. I used to watch how Angelo, the owner of the Lilydale Bakery, would take all kinds of grief from fussy customers without ever losing his friendly smile. Why? Because he never wanted anyone to have a bad experience in his store. Angelo took great pride in his bakery. To him this didn't mean just caring about the bread; it meant creating and maintaining good relationships with his customers and providing a quality product in a friendly, accommodating environment.

Angelo wanted his customers to be satisfied no matter how picky or rude they were. Although I don't know for sure, I could swear Angelo actually enjoyed it when a customer had a problem, because he knew he could find some way to fix it—knew that he could take dissatisfaction and not only turn it into satisfaction but create a return customer as well. Talk about a lesson in customer relations!

I've also worked at other places that didn't take this approach, and I saw how it affected business and employee attitude. Not good. Point being: If you're in the service industry, appreciate the good customers, forget the bad ones, and be as helpful as you can.

recognize their work by thanking them for it! Especially when someone gives you extra help or breaks away to assist you when they were busy stocking shelves or doing inventory. Sure, it's their job—but don't you enjoy being appreciated for doing *your* job?

When I was sixteen, I worked at the Lilydale Bakery (best bread ever!). At least once a day, I would get the picky customer: that one who orders a sandwich special and makes lots of substitutions—don't forget she wants just a little bit of mayo—and eighty-sixes the pleases and thank-yous. I'd think to myself, *Boy, this customer is obnoxious*, and then I'd scowl and make the sandwich without an ounce of pride in my work or consideration for her. (Believe it or not, there is a certain pride in assembling a well-made sandwich that won't fall apart.)

Why was I scowling and huffing? *Because I felt unappreciated.*

Customer's fault? My fault? Answer: both. When someone is rude, you have one rude person, which is bad enough. When the other person responds with rudeness, you've got two rude people. On the other hand, if you can maintain your composure and remain pleasant when you're on the receiving end of rude behavior, often the person acting rude will realize that he or she is being a jerk. If not, at least you didn't waste your energy on being rude in return.

Checking Out

This is really a place where all you can do is wait your turn and pray everything goes smoothly. Small acts of etiquette can go a long way here: Letting someone go ahead of you when they have only one or two items; calling attention to an incorrect bill—even when the mistake is in your favor; and setting line-cutters straight in polite, gentle tones ("I'm sorry, but I think the line starts over there").

INSTANT TIP

Never talk on your cell phone while paying for your purchases at the cash register. When you do this, you're saying to the person ringing you up that as far as you're concerned, he isn't there.

Sometimes people get upset when one of the customers ahead of them has a problem that causes a delay. My advice? Be patient and put yourself in the other person's shoes: We all get a little uncomfortable when we're holding people up.

When the salesperson hands you your receipt, it's important to remember two things:

- **Say "Thank you."**

- **If the salesperson thanks you, say "You're welcome."** Ah, the lost art of *accepting* appreciation. Have you noticed how much trouble people have saying "You're welcome" these days? How many times have you done this: You've gotten great service from someone at a store—I mean *really* great service—and as you're signing the credit card receipt the salesperson says, "Thank you so much for coming in today." Then you (even though you've *already* thanked the person) turn around and say, "Oh no, thank *you*—you were such a help." No, you haven't done anything wrong exactly, but you're implying that the other person's "thank you" is unimportant, and that *your* appreciation of her help is more important. While I don't think anyone would actually be offended by the above exchange, you should always recognize someone's appreciation by saying "You're welcome." Bottom line: *It's okay to acknowledge someone else's thanks.*

The Exit

As you exit the store with packages in hand (or not), say good-bye to that same greeter if she is by the door. Better yet, say, "Have a nice day"—because isn't that a good thing to wish for anyone? (Especially if your job is to hang out by a door all day long.)

SHOPPING SNAFUS

Some fast tips on what you should do when you're confronted with a worst-case scenario—like a salesperson who stares through you as if you don't exist.

- **When a salesperson is rude to you:** Let's face it: Not every member of the service industry is always peachy-keen-hunky-dory-dying-to-help-you-out. Sometimes people have bad days or are just plain rude. If you ask for someone's assistance and they ignore you, or snap at you, or heave a huge sigh that translates into What the hell do you want? then you should either find another salesperson or, in your most patient voice, say "I'm sorry. I was just wondering if you could help me or tell me where I can find someone who can." Usually the person will then unbend enough to assist you or at least direct you to someone else who will.

  If the unresponsive salesperson continues to huff at you or be of no assistance whatsoever, don't try to lecture him on what customer service is really all about. Instead, if you think the situation warrants it, ask to speak with the manager or go search him or her out yourself. Explain the situation and the difficulties you've been having with the salesperson. You don't do this because you think the manager will fire the employee on the spot or reprimand the person in front of you. Rather, you do it so that you can know you've voiced your difficulties in an appropriate way to a manager. Then you move on.

- **When an item is unavailable or unreturnable:** Isn't it annoying? You've driven through traffic, dealt with parking, stood in endless lines, and after all that you still can't find the one thing you *really* wanted—or you're told that you can't return the one thing you *really* didn't want to be to stuck with. *Grrrr.*

To prevent the latter from happening, find out the store's return policy before you make any purchases. (Usually the policy is posted near the cash register.) Remember, too, that items on sale often can't be returned. If you do get caught in a situation where you didn't know the return policy and you can't get your money refunded, many places will be happy to give you store credit in exchange for the returned item. If the store doesn't carry the item you want, ask the sales staff whether they know any other stores that might. As a service to customers, a lot of stores will gladly call their other outlets or even another company's stores to check for the unavailable item.

- **When you have to play the waiting game:** Let's face it: nobody likes to wait. When you're standing in line, time seems to slow *way* down. And as the minutes tick by, it's easy to get into your inner monologue about how you've got all these other things you've got to do, and how absolutely ridiculous it is to be kept waiting so long, and how the clerk is so freaking slow that you could have easily rung yourself up and left by now, and so on and so on.

INSTANT TIP

If you've been working with a salesperson to shop for an item but haven't yet made the purchase, be sure to get her name, and then remember it when you come back to buy the item. (You can also ask for a business card.) Often, salespeople get a commission, or at the very least recognition, for the sales they make. This is why many stores will ask for the name of your salesperson when you're making your purchase. If the person's name slips your mind, give a brief description instead.

Stop. Take a deep breath. Remember that the cashier can see how long the line is and how frustrated people are getting. Chances are, his intent is to provide good customer service to each person in line. So stand patiently and try to think about something else—the Bahamas, for instance. Meanwhile, you can help speed things along by having your cash or credit card ready to go when you reach the register. When your turn finally arrives, be understanding. And always, always remember the importance of *thank you* and *you're welcome*.

CHAPTER 10

THE CELL PHONE

YEAH DUDE, I know . . . Oh, it was awesome. . . . I know. . . . Totally. . . . Yeah, I *know* . . ."

I don't know what it is that he knows, and frankly I don't care—but since I'm stuck next to him in this elevator, one thing *I* know is that I'm going to be hearing all about it for the next dozen floors.

Cell phones make the world wonderfully accessible: Now that we have the entire phone directory at our fingertips anytime we want it, those days of being stranded on a long drive without a gas station or of wondering, *How can I get word to them that I'm going to be late?* are over for good. Kiss good-bye those times you couldn't get hold of a friend at a club—we've got cell phones, baby!

Of course, as with any great device, the opportunities to misuse cell phones are also plentiful. When someone's "Hit Me Baby One More Time" ring tone goes off in the movie theater, it makes us all cringe. But the funny thing is, it's not the cell phone that's creating the disturbance—it's the *person who's misusing it* that's causing the problem. In other words, with power must come the will to control it.

YOU VERSUS YOUR PHONE: WHO'S IN CHARGE?

The most important single guideline of cell phone etiquette is this: Rule your phone, instead of letting it rule you. Remember, it's up to *you* whether your phone and ringer are left on or off, and whether or not you answer each call that comes in. In any given situation, the choices you make will depend on several factors:

- Where am I?

- What am I doing?

- Who's around?

- Do I *have* to take this call right now?

If you're at a store and your items are being rung up by the clerk, are you going to answer a call from your friend? What if it's a workday, and your boss calls while you're eating lunch? Is your ringer going to be switched on when you're walking with your date to a restaurant? When you're riding in an elevator, a subway car, or a bus, are you going to force everyone around you to listen to your half of the conversation?

There are always going to be those times when you're going to want to take an important call, even if you're stuck on a bus or out on a date. The key is always to show consideration and respect for the people around you when making your decisions. (Leave my ringer on or off? Take the call or not?)

FOUR ESSENTIAL CELL PHONE RULES

There are four essential rules for using a cell phone:

1. **TURN IT OFF.** If the ringing of your phone is going to bother the people around you—especially if you're in a meeting, at a play or movie or concert, or in a quiet place like a library or a church—turn your phone off or switch the ringer to silent or vibrate mode.

2. **STEP AWAY.** Whenever you're around other people and you receive or make a cell phone call, move a short distance away so that you can talk without disturbing the people around you. If you're with a group, simply excuse yourself for a few minutes: "Sorry, I need to take this call. I'll be right back." Then keep the call as brief as possible.

3. **DON'T SAY ANYTHING PERSONAL, PRIVATE, OR CONFI-DENTIAL** if you're in a place where others might be able to

---

YOU TALKING TO ME?!

When you're wearing a cell phone headset in public, remember it might not always be obvious to those around you that you're speaking on the phone. If you're standing at a corner waiting for the light to change and, after a long silence, you suddenly burst out with "You've *got* to be kidding!" the person standing next to you will naturally think you're addressing her.

overhear you. Instead, arrange a time to call back when you can speak privately.

4. **WATCH THE VOLUME.** For some reason, people's "phone voices" are always louder than the voice they use in normal conversation. Add to that the noise of a busy sidewalk or the background noise of a public place, and the urge to shout can become overwhelming. But remember—you're the one fighting to hear over the noise, not the person you're speaking with. So give everyone a break, and remember to tone it down.

NEWS FLASH: YOU *DON'T* ALWAYS HAVE TO ANSWER IT

Back in the olden days before cell phones or caller ID, when we used to invite friends over, they never brought their landline phones from home along with them. They sure do bring their cell phones with them

INSTANT TIP

aking a call signals that the person you're with is less important than the person calling. If that's not the impression you want to make, don't take the call. If, on the other hand, you're with other people and you know you'll be getting an important call that you'll have to take, let them know about it ahead of time: "I just wanted to warn you—I'm going to be getting a call from work, and it could take a little while." That way, they won't feel surprised or slighted when you suddenly have to excuse yourself to take the call.

now, however. If you're the type of person whose cell phone rings constantly, keep in mind how difficult it is for the people you're hanging out with to be put on hold every time your phone rings. When you're with friends, use your judgment before reaching for that ringing phone; in fact, think twice about even leaving it on. After all, your caller can always leave a message on voice mail, to be returned as soon as you have a free moment.

When you do decide to break off to take a call, excuse yourself and step away. If the call involves anything other than a very brief conversation, let the caller know that it's not a good time to talk and that you'll call him or her back another time.

THEN WHY WAS YOUR PHONE *ON?*

There you are, sitting in class or at a business meeting, and your cell phone starts to ring. Embarrassed over what to do, you finally answer it. "I can't talk right now," you mutter, "I'm in class—I'll call you back." Half an hour later, feeling a little miffed at your intrusive friend, you return her call: "Why did you call me? You *know* that I have class on Monday until four. It was *so* embarrassing! The professor doesn't like me as it is . . ."

Hold on just a sec! Why was your phone on in the first place? If you're in a class, at a movie theater, dining at a restaurant, or in the middle of a business meeting, you have a reponsibility to turn your phone *off*—or at least mute the ringer. People aren't telepathic, and they have no way of knowing that they've picked an inopportune time to call. Since you *did* know that it was a bad time to receive a call, you could have easily turned off your cell and avoided an embarrassing situation.

Remember: *You're* in control of your cell phone.

CELL TIPS: WHAT TO DO WHERE

If your cell phone rings and you're . . .

- **IN A RESTAURANT.** Excuse yourself from the table and take the call in another room, such as an anteroom, restroom, or lobby. Never disturb your own table and other diners by making or taking a call while sitting at the table. (Some "cell-phone free" restaurants now actually require diners to check their phones at the door.)

- **ON THE STREET.** Be careful not to talk too loudly (see "Four Essential Cell Phone Rules," page 132). And since talking on a phone has been shown to distract people from their immediate surroundings, for safety's sake pay extra attention to where you're walking.

- **AT THE MOVIES.** If there's an all-important call that you absolutely have to take, set your ringer ahead of time to "vibrate," and try to sit in an aisle seat if possible. When your phone rings, quickly excuse yourself to the lobby to answer the call.

- **IN A STORE.** Rather than continue roaming the aisles as you talk (and disturbing other customers), go off to a private corner to take the call. And definitely end the call before you reach the register.

- **IN A CAR OR ON A TRAIN OR BUS.** Since the people traveling with you in a car or on a bus or train are a captive audience, you should restrict yourself to only the most essential calls—let your rehashing of last night's party wait until the trip's over—and keep all phone conversations as short and as quiet as possible. On a train, consider stepping into the vestibule area between train cars to make any lengthy calls. If you're riding in a "quiet car" on a train, keep your phone on "vibrate" and move immediately to the vestibule or to another car if you need to answer a call. Finally, be aware that speaking on a handheld phone while driving is now against the law in many places; so if you need to make or answer a call while you're at the wheel, either pull over or get a headset that will let you talk while leaving your hands free.

VOICE MAIL ETIQUETTE

One great feature of cell phones is voice mail. And believe it or not, there is etiquette involved both in setting up your own voice mail greeting and leaving a message on someone else's phone.

Your Greeting

You'll want your greeting to state either your name or your phone number, so that the person calling will know they've reached you. Many people choose to make "personalized" greetings (I had a friend whose greeting posed the question, "In a fight between the Keebler Elves and Snap!, Crackle!, and Pop!, who would win?"), but before you go this route, realize that anyone who dials your cell phone number will be subjected to your hilarious message. So take a second to think about

ASK LIZZIE: TAG, YOU'RE IT

Q: If I'm returning a call and I get the other person's voice mail, should I still leave a message, or will this just lead to a game of phone tag?

LIZZIE: Playing phone tag is frustrating for everyone involved, and I agree that you run the risk of it whenever you answer a message with a message. To nip the game in the bud, do one of two things: Give the other person a specific time frame when he or she is guaranteed to reach you back—or say that you'll call back at a specific time. Either way, be sure to stick to your word. If your plans change—you're not going to be available when you said you would be, or you won't be able to call when you promised—just call back and . . . leave another message. (Tag—you're it again.)

CRACKBERRIES—THE LATEST WAY TO ANNOY PEOPLE

One up from the cell phone in capability, the BlackBerry and other similar PDAs are a two-edged communications sword: They're wonderfully convenient, but they can also boomerang on you if you're not careful:

- Take one out and start using it in a meeting, and you may have to explain to your boss why you weren't paying attention.
- Store confidential information on one, and you may suddenly discover how easily these devices can be hacked.
- All the rules for cell phone consideration apply here as well.

Finally, before you ask your boss for one, remember: People who get a PDA through work often complain that their bosses are all too eager to use it as a way to reach them when they're off duty—or even on vacation.

---

what Grandma, your boss, or your date will think when they hear your greeting. Remember, too, that most people simply want to leave a message and be done with it. They don't need detailed information about why you aren't answering the phone at this particular moment or twenty seconds of music from your favorite band. For example, a simple: "You've reached Lizzie's voice mail, you know what to do" will do very well.

Leaving a Message

It's simple: Say hello, then state who you are along with your phone number (if you think it's needed), what you want, and suggest a good time for the other person to call you back: "Hey Claudia, it's Lizzie. I was just calling to see if you wanted to go out for a drink. If you do, call me back before 9:30. You can reach me at____. Thanks. Bye."

If you don't bother to leave a message, don't assume the other person will call you back just because he or she sees a missed call from you. While many people do return nonmessage calls, I know others who won't return a call unless the caller leaves a message. By not leaving a message, you set a tone that implies there was nothing important to say anyway.

Finally, if the person you're leaving a message for isn't someone who knows you and your number well, do him a favor and say your number again (slowly) at the end of the message.

Returning Calls

When someone calls you and leaves a message, calling back is the considerate thing to do. So do it, within 24 hours if possible.

TEXT MESSAGING

I love text messaging. With it, you can get a message to someone without causing their phone to ring at an inopportune time, ask a friend a question and let them respond at their leisure, or just shout out a quick greeting to someone without making a big deal out of it.

There are, however, a few text-message etiquette tips to keep in mind:

- Most important, remember that text messaging is a strictly casual affair—usually used as a prelude to a call. If you really have something important or substantial to say, say it over the phone.

- Make sure you're texting to the right phone number! It's very easy to dial the wrong number or select the wrong phone book entry.

- Keep your text messages brief. No one wants to have an entire conversation with you by texting when you could just call him or her instead.

- Don't text-message anything confidential, private, or potentially embarrassing. You never know when someone might be looking over your significant other's shoulder—or worse yet, when your message might get sent to the wrong person (see second item in this list).

- If you text-message someone who doesn't have your phone number, start your message by stating who you are: "Hi—it's Kate (yoga). Chiropractor's number is: 1-802-555-2020. Good luck."

- When you have a chance, respond to a text message with either a text message or a phone call.

- You shouldn't use text messaging when informing someone of sad news, business matters, or urgent meetings, unless it's to set up a phone call on the subject.

- If you receive a text message that was sent to you by mistake, reply explaining that you aren't the intended recipient. You don't have to respond to anything else in the message.

- Finally, remember that as with e-mail, you can't know for sure when the recipient is going to read his or her message—so don't freak out if your text message doesn't get an immediate response.

CHAPTER 11

DINING: A NIGHT OUT
WITH FRIENDS

AVE YOU EVER been out to dinner with a friend who seems to know just what to do, every step of the way? It's not even anything noticeable, really, except that when you eat out together everything seems to go smoothly: He holds doors, he takes everyone's coat, the reservation is always set, and you've never heard him utter a rude or disapproving remark about service. His patience is impeccable, he always knows exactly how to tell the server that the bill is getting split without making it seem like a big deal, and he's so discreet that you can barely tell he just tipped the maitre d' and the parking valet on the way out.

He's so good at dining out, in fact, that his skills seem almost inborn—but I can guarantee you this: He's not a natural. He's been practicing, and his practice is paying off every time he walks into a restaurant. Because whether you plan on chowing down on home-style cuisine in a casual hole-in-the-wall or stepping up to white-linen tablecloths and full place settings, knowing what to expect—and what's expected of you—allows you to be comfortable, relaxed, and in control of any dining situation.

HEADS UP: CHECK YOUR WALLET FIRST

One thing holds true no matter who you are and where you're planning on going: You need money. Before you go, be sure you're carrying enough cash or credit to cover not only the food but also the tax and tips. Don't forget that if you're going to be drinking, there is often a separate liquor tax in addition to your food tax.

If you're worried about affordability, call the restaurant ahead of time to check on their prices—and don't feel shy about suggesting a less expensive restaurant, if necessary: "Hey guys, would you mind going to Chez Pacific instead? I think it's a little more in my price range." Calculating how much you can afford to spend *before* heading to dinner will ensure that you don't suffer the embarrassment of coming up short on your share of the meal.

The next few pages contain virtually everything you'll need to know in order to dine out with confidence and style. Master these basics, and you will enjoy a lifetime of enjoyable, stress-free dining— because once you know what you're doing, the only thing you need to concentrate on is having a great time with your companions and soaking up the atmosphere.

THE NEWLY INDEPENDENT'S GUIDE TO STRESS-FREE DINING

When you're eating out at a nice place, do you sometimes wish you knew a little bit more about the finer points of restaurant dining? Believe me, you're not alone: The process *can* get rather complicated at times—so let's go out to dinner and figure it out together.

Choosing a Date, Time, and Place

When you decide on the spur of the moment to grab a meal or a drink at some casual restaurant or bar—a laid-back place, where you know there'll be room for everyone to squeeze in—it's fine to simply whip out the cell phone and invite whoever you think might be interested: "Hey, a bunch of us are going down to 10th Street Bar and Grill after work. Why don't you stop by?" In this sort of informal situation, if the other person makes it, fine; if not—well, that's fine, too. In fact, casualness is one of the nice aspects of impromptu get-togethers.

If, on the other hand, you have a desire to sit down with some friends in a nice restaurant to enjoy good food, good drink, and good conversation, your natural spontaneity is going to have to give way to some planning. This means picking a specific time and place well ahead of time, pinning down who will be attending, and confirming your plans with your fellow diners once everything is set. If the restaurant where you're planning to eat at is a happening one, you may also need to make a reservation ahead of time.

Scheduling a dinner at least a few days in advance makes it easier to select a time and date that works for everybody, and it also sets the night apart as something special—a date to be looked forward to with anticipation by all parties. Unless you're hosting a meal to celebrate someone's birthday or other milestone (in which case the schedule of the honoree takes precedence) setting the *date and time* is really a matter of finding a slot that works for everyone. The best way to accomplish this is to call or e-mail the people you're planning to dine with a week or two ahead of time, and offer them several possible dates. Feel free to indicate your own preference if you have one: "Hi,

~ HAPPY BIRTHDAY! GOT ANY CASH? ~

If you're organizing a special occasion out at a restaurant or bar to celebrate a friend's birthday or other life or career milestone, you can't expect your friend to pay her own way. It's the group's responsibility to split the honoree's tab among them. On the other hand, it's *not* okay to invite a bunch of friends out to dinner to celebrate your own birthday, and then expect them to chip in for you. If you're the one who suggested the dinner, it's incumbent upon you to offer to pay for your own meal.

Kaitlyn, this is Sarah. Eli and I were thinking it would be fun to meet you and Parker for dinner one night next week. We're hoping Seth and Jill can join us, too. Either Friday or Saturday works best for us—but if neither day is good for you, Thursday's also a possibility."

In this case, it turns out that Parker and Kaitlyn are traveling on Saturday and Jill and Seth both work Thursday nights, but Friday is perfect for everyone. So they're all set for a date.

Picking the *place* also takes a bit of forethought. You'll want to choose a restaurant that everyone is happy with. You may have a spot you're dying to check out—and if so, it's fine to say so: "That new place, Café Lucille, is supposed to be terrific. How does that sound to you?" At the same time, you need to be sensitive to other people's likes and dislikes, as well as any special dietary requirements they might have: "I know that Kaitlyn is a vegetarian, but I hear their salads and *pommes frites* are great!"

If you plan to pay for the meal of the person you're inviting, then the time to make that clear is when you're first extending the dinner invitation: "One other thing, Kaitlyn—in honor of you and Parker moving back to town, Eli and I want to treat you both to dinner."

⟶ DRESSING UP FOR DINING OUT ⟶

Y es, dining out in America has become an increasingly casual affair—but some restaurants can still be pretty strict about what you must wear to make it inside the door. Besides, if you're going to a halfway decent place, you don't really want to show up in an old T-shirt and torn jeans, do you? Above all, you don't want to go to the trouble of setting up a date and making your reservation only to arrive and be told you can't be seated because you aren't wearing a tie or because you have a pair of (admittedly quite expensive) basketball shoes on your feet.

To avoid these and similar embarrassments, keep the following guidelines in mind when you're dressing for dining out in a fine establishment:

- **SKIP THE T-SHIRTS WITH LOGOS OR ILLUSTRATIONS.** When you walk into the restaurant, you want heads to turn because you're a member of such a sharp-looking group—not because people are wondering what mosh pit you just came from.

- **AVOID FLIP-FLOPS.** A little while ago, a national championship women's athletic team was invited to meet and pose for a picture with President Bush at the White House. What was the big news story afterward? The team photo—because it showed several of the otherwise impeccably dressed girls wearing, you guessed it, flip-flops.

- **WEAR DRESS OR CASUAL SHOES.** They may cost $200, and they may be carbon copies of what Michael (or Andre, or A-Rod) wears, but in the maitre d's eyes, those high-tech athletic shoes are still sneakers. So leave 'em at home.

- **WHEN IN DOUBT, WEAR A JACKET AND TIE.** There's no way around this one, guys, so if you're not sure about the restaurant's

CONTINUED ⟶

dress code, do yourself and your companions a favor and play it safe. If you like, you can simply put on a sport jacket and stick the tie in your pocket, to be added when you get to the restaurant, if necessary. (Some restaurants keep spare ties and jackets on hand for lending to unprepared diners—but don't count on this.)

- **LOSE THE BASEBALL CAP.** I know some guys feel naked without it—but the only thing tackier than showing up at a nice restaurant in your Red Sox cap is failing to remove it once you're inside the door.

Making the Reservation

After you've all settled on a date, time, and place, it's *always* a good idea to call the restaurant and reserve a table for the time you've chosen. This is particularly true if it's a special occasion, such as someone's birthday. If you simply show up, you could be in for a long wait—and there's no surer way to take the air out of a nice dinner than spending an hour and a half stuck in a waiting area or at the bar (in which case you'd probably do well to call around and find another restaurant that can take your party sooner).

When you phone the restaurant, let the staff know what time you'll be arriving and how many people are in your party. You should do this even if you don't expect the restaurant to be full: The advance warning will help the restaurant know how many diners to expect and will alert the maitre d' to hold a suitable table for you.

If the restaurant is known to be very busy, it's also a good idea to call and check on available dates and times *before* calling your friends to set up the dinner. If the restaurant is really popular, your choice may be limited to what you can get: "Café Lucille is full up on Saturday, but they have a table for six available on Friday at eight-thirty. How about if we meet there at the bar around eight for a drink?"

When you call to make a reservation, it's also the perfect time to ask about the restaurant's dress code ("Do you require all men to wear a jacket and tie?") and to put in any special requests you might have, such as a birthday cake or a table on the terrace.

If your plans change: If the number of people in your party changes significantly, or if you find you have to cancel the dinner reservation, call the restaurant at least a day in advance to let them know. You should also call ahead to the restaurant that evening if you find you're running more than 15 minutes late—both as a courtesy and to protect your reservation. Often the restaurant staff will be able to hold your table a bit longer or juggle tables to accommodate the time shift.

Confirming With the Group

The person who makes the reservation has an obligation to make sure everyone else attending the meal has the following information:

- The date and time of the dinner

- The name and address of the restaurant

- The name that the reservation is under

- Any dress code requirements

Call or e-mail your friends after you've made the reservation, to confirm the details. Now is also the time to decide if you're going to meet at the restaurant or somewhere else beforehand. Some restaurants won't seat you until your whole party is present, which makes meeting up early a good idea.

Arriving at the Restaurant

If you drive to a restaurant that has valet parking, your first restaurant "etiquette encounter" will be with the person parking your car. Hand him or her the keys, smile, and say "Thank you."

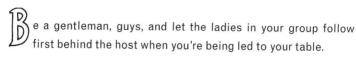

Be a gentleman, guys, and let the ladies in your group follow first behind the host when you're being led to your table.

The next person you'll find yourself face-to-face with will be the maitre d', sometimes called the host or hostess, who will be standing at the entrance to the dining area. If you have a reservation, say, "We have a reservation under the name of . . .". If you don't, simply say, "We'd like a table for six, please."

The first person to arrive should wait for the second, then the two of you can ask the maitre d' to be seated. If the restaurant won't seat you until your whole party has arrived, wait at the bar or in an area where you won't block the flow of traffic until everyone gets there.

What if you aren't happy with the location of your table? If you see another empty table that looks more appealing, there's nothing wrong with politely asking the maitre d', "Would it be possible for us to sit *there*?" The worst thing that can happen is that your request will be turned down.

Pre-Dinner Drinks

It's perfectly cool to order a pre-dinner drink while you're waiting at the bar or if you're seated before the rest of your party has arrived. If you have your drink at the bar, it's customary to tip the bartender and close out your tab before going to your table, unless the bartender or waitstaff have indicated that your drinks have been shifted to your table's bill. (In some restaurants, a waiter may also carry your unfinished drinks to your table for you.)

Who Sits Where?

There are all sorts of traditional ways of deciding who sits where, from the old concept of splitting up the host and hostess to alternating male/female around the table. In today's restaurant world, however, informal seating plans are the rule. Unless somebody is hosting and paying for the entire meal (in which case it's his or her choice where everyone is seated), people can generally choose to sit wherever they want.

That said, there are a few points worth keeping in mind:

- Seats that look out on the restaurant or out a window with a view are considered better seats than those facing the wall. Offering them to your companions is always a thoughtful gesture.

A TIME *NOT* TO TIP

Offering the maitre d' or hostess money when you first arrive at the restaurant to try to obtain a better seat or get seated faster is inconsiderate. Attempting to bribe him or her shows that you don't think too highly of the establishment or the people who work there. After the meal it's a different story, however. While it's not necessary to tip your maitre d', tipping one who has been a particular help to you (working to accommodate an expanded party, for example, or getting you a better table) or especially considerate is a wonderful gesture when done at the end of the night. It shows that you appreciate the good effort he or she made while you were dining—a much more respectful gesture than attempting to "buy" a good effort from him at the start of the night. (See "Tipping 101," page 218.)

INSTANT TIP

ometimes it's okay to be fashionably late—but showing up for a dinner reservation is not one of those times. When you've arranged to meet friends at a restaurant, arriving even five minutes late is pushing it: If the restaurant seats only full parties, your friends could be stuck waiting inside the door for you.

- There's no requirement that you and your significant other be "split up" for the evening. So if you want to sit next to your sweetie, go for it.

- It's perfectly okay to switch seats later on in the meal—after the main course, for example, while you're waiting for dessert to be served—so that more people get a chance to visit with each other. Just make sure that everyone has clean silverware, and take your napkin and drink with you.

Placing Your Food Order

The waiter has taken your drink orders, and is back to know what you'd like to eat. (If your waiter hasn't appeared yet, placing your closed menu in front of you sends the signal that you're ready to order.) When you're part of a group, this always raises that awkward question: Should you order whatever you want, regardless of price, or stick to the more-moderately priced dishes?

If you're paying your own way and have asked for a separate check, you're free to order anything on the menu that you feel you can afford. If you know your group is going to be splitting the check evenly, however, it's only fair to your friends to order moderately. And when you're being treated to dinner, steering clear of the most expensive items is

"EXCUSE ME, WAITER?"

The only times you should send back a plate of food are when . . .

- The dish isn't what you ordered
- The dish wasn't cooked properly (for example, you asked for a rare steak and got one that was well-done)
- The dish tastes like there's something wrong with it
- You find a hair or a pest in your food

always the polite thing to do. (See box, "When Someone Else is Paying," page 152.)

Your waiter will usually start by listing the specials of the day. It's perfectly okay to ask the price of any specials that interest you—in fact, it's a good idea, since specials tend to be on the expensive side. The waiter will then go around the table, taking each person's order for starter dishes and the main course. There's no requirement that you order the same courses as everyone else. If you don't feel like having an appetizer or a dessert, that's fine. Ditto if you'd rather feast on appetizers and skip the entrée. If you want to split an appetizer or an entrée with another person, now is the time to let your waiter know, so they can bring an extra plate. (When you split an entrée, leave the waiter a larger-than-normal tip to make up for your reduced bill—unless the restaurant charges you an extra "plate fee" for the privilege.)

Ordering the Wine

If you're having wine with dinner, the best time to order a bottle is after you've all placed your food order. (See "Selecting the Wine," page 170.) Besides choosing a wine that goes well with the various entrées,

I f you want your bill to be split into separate checks, tell the waiter when you're placing your order—*not* at the end of the meal.

be sure the price of the wine you've picked matches everyone's budget. (There's no faster way to drive up a dinner tab than by ordering a too-expensive vintage.)

As you're glancing over the wine list, be sure also that you're clear on whether you're looking at the half-bottle or whole-bottle side of the menu. I had a very embarrassing dinner out once where my friend Claudia and I ordered a full bottle of very good (and usually very expensive) champagne, thinking we were getting a bargain—only to discover when the check arrived that we'd been looking at the half-bottle price list. Let's just say it really ran up the bill.

When your waiter brings the bottle of the wine to the table, he or she will present it to whoever actually ordered the wine. If this is you, confirm that it's the bottle you chose by looking at the label and then nodding to the server. The server will then uncork the bottle and pour a small amount of wine into your glass. Give the wine a quick sniff and take a sip. If it tastes all right, simply say "That's fine." The server will then pour wine for the entire table, filling the orderer's glass last.

DINNER CONVERSATION

Dining out is all about enjoying good conversation, so this is one area where you want to shine. To be a great conversationalist, all you need to do is follow three simple rules:

- *Listen.* A Good listener gives his full attention to the person he's speaking with. Focus on the words your companion is saying and how he's using those words. No "yessing" and "yeahing" while you're really wondering to yourself whether or not the Yankees lost or why the waiter is taking so long with your drinks—your attention belongs to those who are with you at the table.

- *Respond.* A reply that builds on something the other person just said shows not only that you're paying attention to him but also that you understand and are thinking about what he's saying ("That's so amazing—I love Jane Austin, too! . . .").

- *Maintain eye contact.* By making consistent eye contact with the person you're speaking with, you send the message that she's engaging you with her conversation and that you enjoy her company.

If you're at a table with three other people, make a point of speaking with everyone during the evening. When you're at a table of five or more,

WHEN SOMEONE ELSE IS PAYING

If Sarah and Eli are treating the other couples to dinner, what their guests order suddenly takes on more significance. When someone is taking you out to eat, don't go overboard—even if your hosts tell you to order anything you want. This is not the time to order that big bottle of Veuve Clicquot. But that doesn't mean you have to order the cheapest thing on the menu, either. Take a moderate approach: Order something at a price point you feel comfortable with—just be careful to veer away from the priciest items on the menu.

your primary conversation partners will be the people on either side of you, so try to spend equal time talking with each of them. If one table-mate has been monopolizing you for a while, wait for a natural break in the conversation, then turn and engage the person on your other side.

Two other tips to bear in mind: No matter how good a time you're having, try to keep your volume in check. Surveys have found that people talking or laughing too loudly is the *number-one complaint* among restaurant-goers. And finally, turn off that cell phone before you walk through the restaurant door—and keep it turned off until you walk back out. (See Chapter 10, "The Cell Phone," page 130.)

What Should We Talk About?

- *What's safe:* Certain topics are sure bets to stimulate lively conversation without any risk of ticking people off. These include favorite movies; sports; food and drink; music, including any concerts or shows you've seen recently; hobbies and recreational activities; your job or course work; current events; and news of mutual friends.

- *What's not:* Other topics should be on the table only with friends whom you know well—and even then, they should be handled

~ ASK LIZZIE: ~
"CONVERSATIONAL FOUL"

Q: What should I do if one of my dinner partners tries to engage me in a topic I'm not really comfortable discussing?

LIZZIE: You can shut him off simply by smiling and saying, "Ryan, to be honest, I really don't want to go there tonight. Let's talk about something else instead. . . ."

~ LONE MAN OUT

M y family went to Italy for the thirty-fifth anniversary of my mother's school. We had many dinners to attend and lots of alumni to converse with. I noticed one gentleman seated at our table who no one seemed to know. It turns out he had graduated in a different year from the rest of the group. *Heck,* I figured, *I'd be nervous or bored if that happened to me.* So I started talking to him. He told me about what it was like when he was studying in Rome and what he'd gone on to do in his life. I ended up having a great conversation with him—one that gradually drew others to join in as well, telling stories and comparing professors. I could see how happy he was to have been included. The experience taught me a valuable lesson about socializing: What on earth have you got to lose by simply turning to someone new and striking up a conversation?

with great care. These include politics (always a big one for starting arguments), religion, surgery or medical conditions, money matters, negative or back-stabbing gossip.

THE BILL: WHO PAYS FOR WHAT?

The financial arrangements regarding who's paying for what should *always* be established upfront, when you're first planning the dinner, so that everyone has a clear idea of what's expected. If no one has specified that they're picking up the check, it's usually assumed that the group will split the tab. Exactly how the bill is divided up, however, will depend on the circumstances:

- If it's an informal get-together, you can all make the decision jointly to put everything on one bill or, if some of the group prefers, get separate checks. Either choice is perfectly okay, as long as you decide when you first sit down at the table, before you've actually ordered: "Is it all right if we just put everything on one tab?" "Actually, Jill and I prefer a separate check—we're planning to pay by credit card."

- If you decide on a single check and everyone orders food in the same price range, it often makes the most sense to split the bill evenly among all the diners. A couple of dollars one way or the other is usually no big deal to anyone.

- If, on the other hand, some people in the group order dishes that are significantly more expensive than what their companions have ordered or if some people consume two or three drinks

FIFTY BUCKS FOR A SALAD AND SODA?!

You had a late lunch, so you just order a salad and a soda, while the rest of the table goes for full entrées plus dessert. Then the bill arrives and some genius suggests that everyone split the check evenly.

Gulp. What can you do without looking like a total cheapskate? It's perfectly okay for you to pipe up and say, "Hey, guys, I only had a salad and a soda—how about if I throw in $15 and you all split the rest?" Even if this generates a grumble or two, your feeling that you paid your fair share is preferable to your feeling that you've been ripped off, however unwittingly.

LOVE THAT DOGGIE BAG!

The only times you should *not* ask for a doggie bag are at a business meal and at a wedding reception or some other special function. Other than that, wrap it up, take it home, and enjoy!

---

while others have one or none, the bigger spenders should offer to cover a larger share of the bill: "We should put in an extra twenty dollars—don't forget, we had drinks with dinner while you just had water."

LEAVING THE TIP

In general, waitstaff in the American service industry are paid a lousy hourly wage because their bosses expect them to make up the difference in tips. In addition, these tips often go into a tip pool that's shared by the waitstaff, cooks, buspersons, dishwashers, hosts, and bartenders. So if you don't tip appropriately, you may be shortchanging not only your own waiter but the rest of the employees as well.

Tipping Your Waiter

As a rule of thumb, if the service was fine but not exceptional, leave a respectful tip equal to 15 percent of your food and drink tab. (Remember, you should tip on the subtotal only—not the total, which includes tax.) If the service was really incredible—your server easily handled your substitutions and separate checks and was unfailingly pleasant about it—tip a little extra (20 percent or more). If you feel you were given poor service, instead of leaving no tip or an intentionally tiny amount to "send a message," you should tip in the ten-to-fifteen percent range and definitely speak to the manager about the service on your way out. After all, your boss doesn't dock your pay just because you had a slow day at the office or because you messed up the copy machine—right? Service industry people deserve the same consideration: Always tip. (See "Tipping 101," page 218.)

Tipping the Coat-Check Attendant

Whoever picks the coats up from the coat check should leave $2 for the first coat and $1 for each coat checked after that. If there's no tip jar in sight, hand the tip directly to the coat-check attendant or leave it on the counter with a word of thanks.

Tipping the Parking Valet

If you left your car with the valet parking service, you'll need to pick it up at the end of the meal. This is when you should tip the valet. Give $2 in smaller cities and $3 to $4 in larger cities. And always thank the valet.

A Nice Touch on the Way Out

Always thank any restaurant staff members you encounter on your way out the door. It's a nice way of letting them know that you had a pleasant evening and that you appreciate the service their establishment provided.

Saying Good Night

When you leave your friends, say a sincere thank you for the great evening you had; it's a nice way to let them know that you really appreciated spending time with them.

CHAPTER 12

DINING: THE MECHANICS OF IT ALL

H MAN, you think, *here it comes: the rules.*

Damn straight, here are the rules. Eating can be one gross act, and if you don't believe me, look in a mirror as you eat. (You've got a little . . . yeah . . . there on your cheek . . .)

My great-great-grandmother Emily had a story she loved to tell:

City Suave falls in love with Country Bumpkin and asks her to marry him. Bumpkin now has to meet Suave's city family, and she's terribly nervous at the prospect. Suave lovingly teaches her the order of the courses and everything about utensils, glasses, and plates that she needs to know in order to be well prepared when she dines with his family.

Finally, off to the city they go. At dinner, with the whole family watching her to see what she does, Bumpkin handles herself perfectly. After eating a lovely lobster main course, the plates are cleared and the server brings in small bowls of water and sets them in front of the guests. The others wait for Bumpkin to make a move. Bumpkin glances at the bowl uncertainly—then, instead of dipping her fingers in it, she picks up her spoon and starts drinking the water. Of course, the bowl is actually a finger bowl, used for cleaning up after the messy lobster course. A few snickers can be heard around the table, as everyone looks to Suave's mother to catch her reaction to the glaring faux pas. Without batting an eye, Mother Suave picks up her spoon and starts drinking the water as well.

There are a number of lessons here:

1. Anytime you're unsure of what to do, wait and observe others.

2. Anytime you're the host, show your guests what to do.

3. When a guest makes a mistake, make them feel comfortable, not embarrassed.

4. If you're a guest of honor and other guests are looking to you to start but you're unsure how to proceed, simply say, "I'm terribly sorry, but I'm not quite sure what to do with this."

Making people feel comfortable and considering their feelings when you're with them is what etiquette is all about. That said, however, it also helps to know a few particulars about dining with other people. Two thorny areas in particular can cause people to feel insecure about their table manners: *table settings* and *eating difficult foods*.

UNDERSTANDING THE TABLE SETTING

For those of you who have been dying to know, here it is—everything you'll find at a table setting, and how to use it.

For a casual dinner out (that is, not a formal place setting but not paper napkins, either), you will see and use the following:

- **Salad plate:** Small plate to the left of the forks.

- **Bread plate:** Small plate, placed at the left of the setting, above the forks, sometimes accompanied by a small butter knife.

- **Forks:** You may have one; you may have two. Sometimes they are the same size; sometimes one is smaller than the other. In truth, it doesn't matter, because you can decipher which fork to use based on its placement. Forks on the side of your plate are used during dinner, in "outside in" order (see "The 'Outside In' Rule," page 161). If a fork is placed at the top of your place setting, it's to be used for dessert. If a food item (such as lobster or escargot) requires a special fork, it will be brought out for you.

- **Knives:** Knives are located to the right of your plate. If you order a steak, roast beef, or some other form of red meat, you'll most likely be brought a steak knife when the entrée arrives.

- **Spoons:** Your spoon is placed to the right of your knife. If two spoons appear, one to the right of the knife and one across the top of the table setting, the one to the right should be used for an appetizer such as soup, while the one above the plate is for dessert.

THE "OUTSIDE IN" RULE

hoosing the right utensil or plate to use is the easiest thing in the world. Just go from *the outside in*. If salad or appetizers are being served before the main course, use your salad fork (usually the smaller of the two forks), which will be set to the left (outside) the fork you'll use for the entrée. If you choose not to have an appetizer, the server will take away your first fork, leaving you with the entrée fork on the outside, ready for your use.

- *Glasses:* Your water glass will appear on the right side of your table setting, at a 45-degree angle off the tip of your knife. Any wine glasses will be set to the right of the water glass or will be brought to the table when wine is ordered.

- *Napkin:* Your napkin lies either under your fork(s) or is folded in the center of the place setting.

- *Coffee cup and saucer:* Coffee served during a meal requires that the cup and saucer be set out before dinner. The coffee cup and saucer are set on the right side of your place setting. If coffee is being served after the meal, then it will be brought out to the table after plates are cleared.

GETTING FOOD TO YOUR MOUTH

The two dining styles considered acceptable when it comes to table manners are continental and American. The following guidelines apply to both right- and left-handed eaters:

THE *b* AND *d* RULE

$\mathcal{S}$ometimes at banquets and large gatherings (particularly weddings), table settings can get tight, making it difficult to know
which bread plate and glasses are yours. (In fact, Emily herself was
always forgetting which bread plate she was supposed to use.) To
help you remember, here's the easiest trick in the world; it can be
executed discreetly under the table whenever you need to double-
check yourself:

On both hands, hold your thumb and index fingers together to
make an *O* and let your last three fingers stick straight out. Your left
hand will look like a *b* and your right will look like a *d*. The *b* is for
bread (bread plate on the left). The *d* is for *drinks* (water glasses and
wineglasses on the right). Now you know which glasses to drink
from and which bread plate to use.

In continental dining, the diner takes the fork in his left hand and
the knife in his right. He cuts his meat or vegetable with the fork tines
down, then uses the knife to push the bite-sized portion onto the fork.
He places the knife on the plate while he lifts the fork to his mouth to
take a bite (tines down).

In the American version, the diner takes the fork in her left hand
and the knife in her right. She cuts a bite-sized portion of food and
places the knife on the plate, then transfers the fork with the food on
it to her right hand and brings the portion to her mouth (tines pointing up).

Both methods are completely correct; it's totally up to you which
style you prefer to use. *How* you grip your utensils as you cut *does* matter, however. Gripping the fork in your fist as if you have stabbed the
meat in order to kill it is *not* the way to go. We have opposable thumbs
for a reason. The fork and knife are held the same way to cut food:
Between your middle and forefingers and your thumb, with your

~ TOP TEN TABLE MANNERS ~

1. Chew with your mouth shut.

2. Avoid slurping, smacking, blowing your nose, or other gross noises. (If necessary, excuse yourself to take care of whatever it is that you need to take care of.)

3. Don't use your utensils like a shovel or as if you've just stabbed the food you're about to eat.

4. Don't pick your teeth at the table.

5. Remember to use your napkin at all times.

6. Wait until you're done chewing to sip or swallow a drink. (The exception is if you're choking.)

7. Cut off only one piece of food at time.

8. Avoid slouching and don't place your elbows on the table while you're eating (though it is okay to prop your elbows on the table while conversing between courses).

9. Instead of reaching across the table for something, ask for it to be passed to you.

10. Always say "excuse me" whenever you leave the table.

---

thumb slightly farther back to keep the utensil balanced. The handle of the knife or fork is placed in the palm of your hand. As you cut, the fork is held between the middle finger and thumb while the forefinger applies pressure along the back of the fork in an effort to keep the food from slipping. At the same time, use your forefinger on the top of the knife to apply pressure to the blade.

THE OTHER STUFF

Now let's find out how to use the rest of the place setting.

Eating Bread from the Bread Plate

When bread is being served, you may take a piece and place it on your bread plate. As the butter comes around, use your butter knife

⸺ ASK LIZZIE: MAY I BEGIN? ⸺

Q: Once I'm served, how soon can I begin eating?

LIZZIE: The polite thing to do, especially on a date, is to *wait until you're both served* before starting. With a large group of friends, you can *start after three people have been served*. At a more formal event or situation (when visiting your significant other's parents, for example), it's best to *wait until your host or hostess starts eating* or until your host tells you it's okay to start. The rule in the Post house is: Start eating while it's hot. Once, when I was twelve, I was at a friend's house and made the unfortunate mistake of asking my friend if I could start eating even though her parents hadn't sat down to the table yet. She said, "Yes, of course." Her father, however, had wanted to say grace first and was astonished that Emily Post's great-great-granddaughter would dare start before others. I never lived it down—and have never since begun eating without first asking the head of the table.

or, in lieu of one, your dinner knife to take a pat of butter and place it on your bread plate. Break off a small piece of bread and use your knife to butter the piece while holding it against the bread plate. You can then use your fingers to bring the piece of bread to your mouth to eat. The butter knife should lie across the bread plate when you're not using it.

Drinking Wine from a Wineglass

Hold white-wine glasses by the stem so that your hand doesn't warm the wine. Hold red-wine glasses with the goblet cupped in your hand to help warm the wine. If you're left-handed, it's okay to put the glass down to the left of your place setting after you take a drink of water or wine.

Eating from Your Salad Plate

Most often, salad is served as a separate course. Once in a while, you'll find that the salad has been preset at the table to the left of the forks. If there's no plate in the middle of your place setting, you can move the salad in front of you if you prefer.

HOW DO I EAT THAT?

Your friends probably won't care if you sop up the leftover spaghetti sauce with a piece of bread clutched in your paw. But if you use your hand instead of a fork when you're out to lunch with your boss, you might raise some eyebrows. Some foods present us with serious challenges that can shake our confidence as diners. Here is a sampling of foods that can be particularly difficult to eat, along with some tips for taming them:

Sushi and Sashimi

When you eat sushi and sashimi, the sashimi (thinly sliced, raw, bone-less fish) is usually served first. Sashimi is eaten by dipping it in a wasabi-and-soy mixture using chopsticks. If your chopstick skills are less than stellar, you may also use your fork and knife.

When eating sushi (raw fish, rolled or served on top of sticky rice), you can use either your fingers or chopsticks to dip the fish side of the sushi into the sauce provided and then eat it. (This way, the rice doesn't break up as you raise the sushi to your mouth.)

Spaghetti

If you jab your fork into the center of your plate, you can probably twist the whole bowlful of noodles onto your fork. Don't go there: instead, take a few strands near the edge of your plate and turn your fork tines against the plate again and again to twist those up into a neat little bunch. If you have a few hanging strands, bring the fork to your mouth and, as you begin to chew, bite the strands off so that they fall onto your plate.

If you like to use a spoon when eating spaghetti, take a few strands on your fork and then twirl the fork against the spoon to wrap the noodles around the tines. You may also cut your noodles with a fork and knife—but cut off a small portion at a time, as opposed to cutting up the whole bowlful at once.

Shrimp

When shrimp is served as an appetizer, as in shrimp cocktail, you may use the small fork (shellfish or oyster fork) to eat the shrimp in one bite, provided it's small enough. If the shrimp is on the large side, use your fork to lower the shrimp to the plate the shrimp cocktail is served on and then cut it, before dipping it in sauce and eating it. If you are with friends and are confident you won't make a mess, you can use your fingers to eat the shrimp. If shrimp is passed around as hors d'oeuvres, you may also use your fingers to eat it.

Sauce and Bread

In a casual setting or when eating with friends, it's fine to use your bread to sop up some of the leftover sauce from a meal. However, you should use your fork to hold the bread while you're sopping and eating. This approach should not be used at a business meal, and should be used with discretion when with your significant other's parents or other VIPs. If you're not sure whether to sop or not, err on the conservative side.

Olives With Pits

In many salads and dishes you'll encounter olives with the pits still in them. Use your fork to bring the olive to your mouth, then discreetly use your fingers to remove the pit from your mouth and set it on the side of your plate.

Mussels, Clams, and Oysters

With shellfish, you'll usually be provided with a small shellfish fork (also known as an oyster fork) to get the meat out of the shell. With clams and oysters served raw on the half shell, you can slurp (great word!) them by holding the edge of the shell to your mouth and letting the body slide into your mouth. (*Note*: They are fabulous when eaten this way, but this technique can be considered a bit crude; in a less casual setting, it's best to use your fork unless your host is doing otherwise.)

Lobster

There's a reason they give you a bib—lobster is messy. Hold the lobster steady with one hand while twisting off the claws with the other; then place the claws to the side of your plate. Use your claw cracker to break the claws and remove the meat inside with your fork or lobster pick. Dip the bite-sized pieces of meat in the butter or sauce that's provided.

The lobster's tail is usually split down the middle so that you can access the meat easily with your fork. You can also tear off the small lobster legs and break them apart at the joints; then bite each leg while sucking the meat from the open end. (This is my favorite part of the lobster.) Place empty shell pieces into the large bowl or platter provided; if one isn't provided, just set them to the side of your plate as neatly as you can. After finishing something this messy, use the "wet nap" offered by the waiter or excuse yourself to clean up in the restroom.

Escargot

When escargot is served in its shell, use snail tongs to hold the round shell with the open end up while you use your small fork to remove the snail and eat it. When served without its shell, such as on toast, escargot is eaten with a knife and fork.

Cherry Tomatoes

Cherry tomatoes can be tricky little suckers because they squirt so easily. Either spear the tomato and cut it in half—which can be a procedure approaching surgery—or use your fork to lift the entire tomato to your mouth and eat it. In doing this, you must, must, *must* keep your lips closed. Otherwise, you run the risk of spraying the entire table with cherry tomato seeds and juice when the tomato bursts.

Asparagus

For a long time now, asparagus has been one of the only areas of dispute between my parents. My mother grew up eating it as a finger food, while my father grew up eating it with a knife and fork. Here's the rule: If asparagus is served firm and without a sauce, it may be eaten with your fingers. If the asparagus is served with a sauce or seems limp, it's best to eat it with your knife and fork. In a business or formal setting, always use a knife and fork.

Artichokes

Artichokes are *always* a finger food. Pluck off a leaf and dip it in whatever sauce is provided. Then bite down on the leaf and pull it through your teeth so that the meat and sauce slide into your mouth. Place the rest of the leaf on the side of your plate or in a bowl or plate provided. Continue this until you've reached the soft center leaves or the inedible thistle-like choke. Use your knife to slice off the remaining leaves and stringy choke to get to the heart. Cut the heart into bite-sized pieces and dip each bite into the sauce.

WOULD YOU CARE FOR SOME WINE?

Wines can be a bit intimidating. So here's a quick blitz on selecting and drinking wines.

Refusing a Glass

If wineglasses are set out for dinner, simply turn yours upside down to indicate you won't be drinking. You may also say "No, thank you" when the server comes to pour. If you're in the middle of a conversation, cover your glass with your hand to let the waiter know that you don't wish to have any wine.

Pouring the Wine

You may be asked to pour a glass of wine for someone at your table. When pouring white wine, fill the glass about two-thirds of the way; with reds, fill the glass about halfway. As you tilt the neck up at the end of pouring, turn the bottle slightly so that the last few drops slide along the rim, as opposed to dripping onto the table or in someone's lap.

Selecting the Wine

If the restaurant offers wine, the choices may be listed on the menu or presented to you as a separate wine list. When it's time to select the wine, you can always defer to someone else by saying "I'd love to, but I know so little about it—I think I'll let you select the wine instead." Better still, take some time to learn more about ordering wine yourself. (See "Ordering the Wine," page 150.) To get you started, here is a quick list of foods and the wines that generally match up well with them.

FISH, MILD (Catfish, Flounder, Sole, Tilapia)
Whites Chablis, German Riesling, Loire Sauvignon Blanc (Sancerre, Pouilly-Fumé)

Light Reds Dry rosé, Beaujolais, lightest Pinot Noir

FISH, OILY (Mackerel, Salmon, Swordfish, Tuna)
Whites New Zealand or Loire Sauvignon Blanc (Sancerre, Pouilly-Fumé), Chenin Blanc, Gewürztraminer, white Burgundy

Light Reds Pinot Noir, Beaujolais, Barbera, Loire Cabernet Franc

SHELLFISH

Whites Loire Sauvignon Blanc (Sancerre, Pouilly-Fumé), Muscadet, dry Chenin Blanc

OYSTERS

Whites Chablis, Austrian Gruner Veltliner, dry sparkling wines, dry German Riesling

POULTRY

Whites German or Alsace Riesling, Chardonnay, Pinot Blanc

Reds Australian Shiraz, California Syrah, Zinfandel, Pinot Noir

PORK

Whites French Chardonnay, Chenin Blanc, German or Alsace Riesling

Reds Pinot Noir, Cabernet Franc, Chianti, Spanish reds (Rioja)

BEEF AND LAMB

Reds Cabernet Sauvignon, Merlot, Rhône reds, Zinfandel

VEAL

Whites German Auslese Riesling, Alsace whites, Rhône whites

Reds Loire Cabernet Franc, Pinot Noir, Chianti, Spanish red (Rioja)

GAME

Reds Burgundy, Rhône reds, Australian Shiraz, Zinfandel

GAME BIRDS

Reds Cabernet Sauvignon, amarone, Burgundy, Rhône reds

PASTA WITH RED SAUCE

Whites New Zealand Sauvignon Blanc

Reds Barbera, Chianti, Zinfandel, Loire Cabernet Franc

PASTA WITH CREAM SAUCE

Whites Soave, Pinot Grigio, Sauvignon Blanc, champagne

INDIAN, CAJUN, AND OTHER SPICY FOODS

Whites German Gewürztraminer, German Riesling, Chenin Blanc, Sauvignon Blanc

Reds Beaujolais, Barbera, Pinot Noir, rosé

HOW DO I . . . ?

Cut My Food?

One bite at a time. Always.

Pass Food Around the Table?

The whole pass-to-the-right thing is really just to ensure that there is some type of guideline. Food is always passed in one direction to avoid having someone end up with two dishes at once. You can either hold the platter for the person you are passing to while she takes her food or, if the platter seems easy to hold and serve from, you may simply pass it to the guest next to you once you've taken your share. Remember to take a small enough portion so that there's plenty left for everyone.

When you pass something that has a handle (such as a gravy boat), pass it with the handle side toward the person you are passing to, so that she can take it easily.

Season My Food?

I like my food a little saltier than most. Unless I've cooked it myself, however, I *always* taste it first before adding salt. It's considered insulting to the chef to automatically assume that something needs to be seasoned. Taste first; then season.

Use a Dipping Bowl?

Often foods are dipped in sauces. If there is a dipping bowl for the whole table, try not to *double-dip* (that is, don't take a bite out of a piece of food, then dip the same piece back into the community sauce). If, however, you have your own dipping bowl, you may double-dip as much as you want. Some foods like oysters are easier to handle if you spoon a small portion of the sauce onto the food before eating it. Other foods, such as shrimp, are easier to eat when you use your fork to dip the food into the sauce. Things such as chips and salsa or artichokes are dipped into the sauce by hand and eaten as a finger food. When in doubt, serve yourself some sauce from the communal bowl. Then you can double-dip to your heart's content without grossing anyone out.

Use a Finger Bowl?

A finger bowl is a small bowl of water that is brought out after eating a somewhat messy meal like lobster or after a finger-food dish. When the bowl is placed in front of you, dip your fingers gently in the bowl and then dry them on your napkin. If you really want to get stuffy about it, only dip one hand at a time.

Deal With an Unpleasant Experience in the Mouth?

If something that tastes funky or foul ends up in your mouth, you can raise your fork to your mouth and subtly use your tongue to remove the object from your mouth and place it on your fork. Then place the item to the side of your plate. Never place the item in your napkin—it's too easy for it to fall out, and stain your clothes or end up on the chair. The idea is try to keep your actions unnoticed, and let your conversation and company take center stage. And as a former busperson in a restaurant, I can tell you from painful experience that it's gross to clear a table and squeeze someone's chewed-up unpleasant experience in your hand as you gather the napkins or have it stain your work clothes when it comes tumbling out.

Let the Waiter Know There's Something in my Soup?

If you discover an insect or a hair in your food, try not to make a big deal of it (especially if you're eating at someone's house). Instead, put your fork or glass down, and wait to signal the server to get you a fresh plate or glass. If you are in someone's home, simply remove the foreign object, set it to the side of your plate, and (if you aren't overly grossed out), continue eating. You do *not* want to mention to your host in the middle of a dinner party that you found something gross in the food. No sirree.

Refuse a Dish?

First of all, try a bite (as my mother would always say). It's always polite to sample a dish, even if it looks unappealing. If you still don't care for the dish, just don't finish it. But if you know you can't stand a certain food or you are allergic to it in some way, you can refuse it by simply saying "No thank you."

Eat Unforkable Food?

If you have a piece of food that you just can't seem to snag with your fork, try not to use your fingers. Instead, use a piece of bread or your knife as a pusher.

Signal That I'm Finished?

Imagining your plate as a clock, set your utensils on the plate so that both handles are resting on the numeral 4. Then leave your plate exactly where it is. Pushing it away is not considered polite.

FOOD IS IMPORTANT; PEOPLE ARE MORE IMPORTANT

Finally, don't forget to have fun: Engage your fellow diners, and enjoy the blissful community of dining in a warm, hospitable environment. When you do, the food and the manners will take care of themselves.

CHAPTER 13

SOCIALIZING: FROM ETIQUETTE WITH FRIENDS TO MEETING NEW PEOPLE

NOWHERE IS ETIQUETTE more valuable than when you're out making your way through the many parties, group hangs, bars, and clubs of this world. Etiquette lets you float effortlessly through any social scene, meeting the people you want to meet and having a great time with them: All you need to do is remember to *think* about what you're doing and how your actions are affecting the people you're with.

KNOW WHAT YOU'RE LOOKING FOR

When I found myself single again after a number of years, I'd go out to bars and parties with my friends, who were introducing me to whole new crowds of people. And I can remember asking myself as I was flirting with someone: *What am I looking to get out of this?* Once I realized that I couldn't begin to figure out what I wanted, I knew this might not be the time to be looking for any kind of serious relationship.

You, on the other hand, might be searching for a lasting relationship. Or maybe you're not looking for monogamy but you'd still like to meet some fun people to date. The point is, you should get clear on what you're in search of *before* you start looking—then be honest about it with yourself and the people you encounter. That's the best way to avoid misunderstandings and hurt on both sides.

GO WHERE THE PEOPLE ARE

In the course of researching this book, one interviewee asked, "Where can I meet people? I mean, I just don't know where to go!"

If you have an established social circle, then you probably have a whole collection of regular hangouts where you spend time with your friends and have plenty of opportunities to meet new people. But if you're on your own—maybe you've moved to a new city, for example—and you aren't in a setting that lends itself to making social contacts (such as school, or a job working alongside lots of other young people), meeting new people can sometimes be difficult. Don't worry, though—they're out there. In fact, you could meet your next date literally anywhere. Think about all the environments and activities where you can make connections with people: at work, through other friends, in bars, at the gym, in cooking or other interest-related classes, on sports teams, even sitting reading a book at a café. There are an endless number of places where you'll bump into people. You just have to take yourself there.

The only real rule here is this: if you sit around at home all the time, you'll never meet *anyone*. So join a gym, take a class, go to a friend's party—but whatever you do, get out of the house. At the very least, you'll make a few new friends.

FIND A WAY TO BREAK THE ICE

"I need to know how to break the ice with a person I'm interested in," said another one of our interviewees. "What kinds of questions should I ask?"

If you're bold, you can simply walk up to a stranger, put out your hand, introduce yourself, and say, "So, what are you up to tonight?" The truth is that other than this sort of direct approach, anything you say will sound like a line or come off as lame. So you might as well just accept this fact and go with it. I've met many guys who started off with a lame line but who eventually turned out to be impressive.

That being said, there are a few tired come-on lines that really should be retired. Think about what you're *really* saying when you trot out these clunkers:

- *"What are you drinking?"* Translation: "I'll buy you a drink." As an opening line, this can come across as a little forward. Instead, offer to buy a drink ("Can I get you the next one?") after a conversation has started up, when you notice the other person has finished their drink.

- *"Haven't we met before?"* Translation: "I definitely want to start a conversation, but I'm not confident enough to just jump in. Instead, I had to fake a potential connection."

- *"You're hot."* Translation: "I want to pick you up."

- *"You're gorgeous."* Translation: "You're a high-quality pickup."

Want a better way to go? Try this:

- **"Hi, I'm Claudia."** Translation: "I'm putting myself out there and making contact, and I don't need to compliment you or pull some stunt to do it." If the other person introduces himself and you respond with a question, bingo—you've got a conversation going.

KEEP THE CONVERSATION GOING

"Umm. . . . umm . . . umm."

Searching for something to say? People tend to get nervous when they have to talk to someone they don't know very well. But here's a secret: The person you're talking to doesn't know you well, either, so you're probably both feeling nervous. How do you handle the situation? Easy: Start off with a basic question, like, "What do you do for a living?" If you then really *listen* to the person's answer, you'll easily find an opening for a follow-up question:

"What do you do for a living?"

"I just graduated college. I've been applying for jobs in marketing."

"Is that what you studied?" (*There's the follow-up question. So easy.*)

"No, I was a studio art major, actually. But I want to put my art skills to work at an advertising agency or something like that."

"Really? I have a friend who's working with JMP. Did you try applying there?"

"Yeah, I did, but they aren't hiring right now. So what do *you* do for work?"

Once you start talking to someone, all you really have to do is listen. By doing this, you're actually telling this person a lot of positive things about yourself. For one thing, you're letting them see that you're interested. And by learning more about the other person (usually the

HOW TO BOW OUT GRACEFULLY

$\mathcal{S}$uppose you've been stuck for the past ten minutes talking to a perfectly nice person who has cornered you and filled you in on everything there is to know about soy farming—fine for ten minutes, but not for the next half hour. How to politely break away? Here a few possible approaches:

- "I'm terribly sorry, but I'm here with other people tonight and I have to get back to them. But it was a pleasure meeting you." (You haven't lied, and you've left on a pleasant note. What more can you ask for?)

- "Excuse me, I have to run to the bathroom." (The key thing to note here is that you *didn't* promise to come back and continue the conversation. Again, you're not lying—as long as you make sure to at least duck into the facilities before moving on.)

- "Pardon me, I see someone I need to talk to." (A little more brazen, plus it immediately commits you to a new conversation partner.)

- "It was lovely talking to you. I'm going to check out the bar/buffet table/band/whatever." (An all-time favorite, this line gets you completely off the hook—unless, of course, the other person pipes up, "Good idea—I'll join you!")

goal in the first place), you're demonstrating that you aren't completely self-absorbed. Finally, you're showing that you're confident enough to talk to people you don't know without losing an ounce of your poise, wit, and charm.

ETIQUETTE AND FRIENDS

A great deal of our socializing time is spent with our friends—the people in our lives whom we know best, and who respect and accept us just as we are. Take a moment right now to think about what makes your closest friends, well, close. What exactly do you appreciate about them?

"They listen to me and think about what I'm saying."

"Instead of judging me, they try to understand me."

"I value the fact that they remember me when I'm not around—like when a friend will come back from a trip and say 'I thought of you when we went scuba diving . . . You would have loved it!'"

"When I need help, my friends are there for me."

People who treat us well, whom we can talk to, who interest us, who share our interests—these are the people who become our friends. Friends are important, which is why it's also important never to take our friends for granted but instead to treat them with consideration, respect, and honesty at all times. When we forget etiquette in our friendships, we run the risk of losing our friends. When we use etiquette in our friendships—being sure to return a phone call, giving an honest but tactful opinion, inviting the other person to come along on an activity, remembering a birthday or other important date—those friendships grow stronger. In this way, good friendships grow into life-long bonds.

THE GOOD FRIEND

There are lots of ways you can show your friends that you know how much they mean to you:

- *Listen.* The greatest friends know how to listen well. They process what you say, and form questions and opinions based on what you're saying. Rather than jumping in with a story about themselves or offering advice you didn't ask for, they *respond* to what you're saying.

LINE ETIQUETTE

There will always be VIPs, people who are "on the list," and employees who get escorted into bars and clubs without having to wait in line. The rest of us just have to be content to wait sometimes. And by that, I mean *no cutting.* I've been that person who couldn't make it down to the club fast enough, and I know how unbelievably frustrating it is to have to wait an extra half hour when your friends are already inside. So I don't really mind letting that *one* person in. It's when the one person becomes two or three—or, worse yet, a group of four or five jumps the line—that we have a problem.

Yes, typically bouncers are on the lookout for such things. This still doesn't mean, however, that you have license to try and sneak two or three people in line when his back is turned. It's inconsiderate to the people behind you—and you know (come on, admit it) that you get annoyed when people do it to you.

- *Reciprocate.* Reciprocating a friend's invitations shows that you had a good time with him or her, and that you're thinking about what might make another great time.

- *Respect your friends' decisions.* A good friend understands that two friends will sometimes see things differently. If you're asked to give advice on lifestyles, relationships, or work, know that in the end, it's your friend's life and the decision is up to him or her—even if you don't agree with the decision.

- *Show that you care.* A good friend cares about what happens to other friends, and, no matter how crazy life gets, makes an active effort to keep up with what's going on in their lives. When you call to say hi or drop someone an e-mail, it makes your friends feel great to know you're thinking of them.

ETIQUETTE AND ALCOHOL

Whenever drinking is involved, our inhibitions are lowered. For some people, this kind of liberation opens them up and makes them more social. For others it has the reverse effect of making them *less* desirable to be around. In fact, the way other people handle alcohol will probably influence your decisions on who you socialize with.

More than we realize, alcohol can change us—so it's critically important to think about who we are and how we act when we're consuming it in public.

WHERE ARE THOSE BEERS? THE ETIQUETTE OF BUYING A DRINK

First you try to snag the bartender's attention with some eye contact and a smile. Nope. Then maybe you hold your credit card or cash a little more visibly. Nada. Lean forward a bit more. Zilch. Welcome to Friday or Saturday night out, ladies and gentlemen, when getting a drink can be a long and difficult task at times. But for all you thirsty pub-crawlers out there, I have good news: If you remember the following simple etiquette tips, you will greatly increase your chances of getting that Cosmopolitan (or Heineken, or Jack) sooner rather than later.

- Although it's their job to serve you, bartenders and servers are not your personal staff. They are busy, stressed, and sober, while everyone around them is having fun and drinking.

- The bartender has to make drinks not only for everyone at the bar, but for the waitstaff's customers as well.

- When you're drinking, it's easy to forget your "pleases" and "thank yous," but they're still very important. So use them, and use them sincerely.

INSTANT TIP

Whether you're in a down-and-dirty tavern or an upscale watering hole, always tip the bartender at least 10 to 15 percent of what you spend on alcohol—and never less than a dollar.

~ ASK LIZZIE: GETTING HIT ON ~

Q: When a stranger starts hitting on me, how can I politely tell him to leave me alone?

LIZZIE: Let's face it—when you're at a club or bar, you're bound to run into people who are out looking for some action, or at least a phone number. As a female, I completely understand the uncomfortable feeling that results when a stranger tries to strike up a leading conversation. On the other hand, I also know how hard it can be to approach someone you don't know. Bottom line—there's absolutely no need to be rude in rejecting an offer to talk or buy you a drink. If you don't want the attention, just smile and say, "Sorry, but I'm really not interested."

- The more pleasant and patient you are (while still making your presence known), the faster you'll be served.

- If you act like a jerk, the bar can kick you out without a second thought.

ACCEPTING COMPLIMENTS

"Those are really great pants!" "Why, thank you."

"You smell amazing." "Thanks."

"I saw you dancing, and you looked great out there." "Thank you!"

"That shirt looks fabulous on you." "Thanks a lot."

"You're a stunning woman." "*Thank* you."

It's not conceited to accept a compliment, and accepting a compliment doesn't mean you have to have a conversation or drink with the

— INSTANT TIP

M y aunt taught me always to keep a drink in hand. She explained that it's a great way to refuse someone's offer to buy you a drink. You can just say, "Thanks for the offer, but I'm all set." (The beverage doesn't have to be alcoholic, either.)

person who gave it to you. All you have to do is thank the other person—end of story. Unless, of course, you want to keep the conversation rolling . . .

When you're the one being gutsy and giving the compliment, remember that honesty and sincerity will go much farther than cheesy lines or unasked-for physical contact. In fact, sometimes the best thing you can do is to drop a compliment on the person and then just let them be. I know I'm intrigued when someone walks up to me, gives me a compliment, and then continues on with their night—because then I know that the compliment was purely a nice gesture, born of honesty.

CHAPTER 14

DATING: FOR REAL

WHEN, IN THE COURSE OF conducting research for this book, people were asked for their thoughts about dating, they responded with more questions than answers:

- "How do I break the ice with a person I'm interested in?"

- "What's appropriate to wear on a date?"

- "When I'm on a date, how open and honest should I be? What if I'm too blunt?"

- "Should I act shy, rather than risk talking about myself too much?"

- "Why didn't he laugh at that joke I made?"

Think we're all still just a little insecure about the world of dating? The truth is, the dating world, especially in college, has changed. For one thing, it's not as formal as it used to be. Increasingly, we are forming relationships with people we've already gotten to know through our social circles, rather than through a series of structured "dates." (See "Pack Dating," page 189.) And though there are conservatives and liberals within the dating world when it comes to sex, our age group increasingly "hooks up" for a while, and *then* moves into dating or a relationship. Even when people do arrange dates, a girl is just as likely as a guy to pop the question and pay for dinner (or at least offer to pay for her share).

Another change is that when people date nowadays, they aren't necessarily looking for a long-term commitment. In fact, some people have resolved *never* to get into a long-term commitment and are thus perpetually playing the field. We've also seen the emergence of online dating, speed dating, and dating services, all designed to help take the sting out of rejection and, in some cases, give would-be daters a sugar coating of anonymity.

Let's just say the dating world has changed since my great-great-grandmother Emily wrote the book. Don't think, however, that etiquette doesn't still find its way into the dating scene: Whether you're on a first date or out with your longtime significant other, there are always potentially awkward situations that can sneak up on you. When

LADIES, SPEAK UP!

I'm saying it simply because it needs to be said: *Women can ask men out.* So don't be shy, ladies. Are you worried about what to say or that you're being too forward? Don't be. Instead, try this: The next time you're talking to a guy you're interested in and you spot a good opening, say something like: "Hey, want to do dinner at my place Thursday night?" Trust me—if he's interested, he'll be psyched you took the initiative.

you have your etiquette principles at the ready, you can relax and enjoy your date's company, knowing you have the confidence and skills to deal with whatever comes your way.

PACK DATING

There's a lot of talk about the current "pack" mentality of dating. Apparently, we newly independents tend to meet the people we date through crowds of friends who intermingle by going out in groups. In fact, more than three-quarters of the people who responded to the Post Dating Survey said that they had met and started dating someone à la pack.

So, how exactly does it work if you're interested in someone you've been hanging out with in a pack? Usually this involves a new arrival to the group. If you're in college, the start of the school year always shakes up every group a bit, as it gains a new member or two or, sadly, loses one to graduation, transfer, or a difficult schedule. If you hang out with people from your job, a new arrival to your office may strike a spark. Or maybe you meet someone in your local soccer league who seems cool to hang out with—or a relationship splits up, and two previously unavailables suddenly become available.

Whenever groups shift, or you feel something new for someone you already know, or you start a new activity, this gives you the opportunity to date someone by first getting to know him or her. If you have your eye on someone you're already hanging out with, think about some special places, events, or fun things you can do that would be of interest to both of you—places where your group as a whole wouldn't necessarily go. Maybe there's a gallery you'd like to check out. You could see if any bands that your crush is interested in are playing in town soon. You can even just suggest coming over to watch a football game or a movie at your house.

WHERE SHOULD WE GO?

D ates don't always have to involve a show or dinner out. Movies, plays, and concerts all make for great entertainment, but unless you plan on hanging out before or after the show, they limit your chance to talk with and get to know the other person. And while sharing a meal is a great vehicle for conversation, it's far from the only one. In fact, once you get your imagination going, picking out something to do that's interesting, different, and fun can be downright . . . romantic!

Here are a few suggestions to get the ball rolling:

- Tickets to a sporting event
- Picnic
- Gallery opening
- Miniature golf
- Fairs or carnivals
- Something crazy like skydiving (but only if you've heard the person talk about how desperately they want to do it!)
- A walk

Whatever approach you take, the fact that you already know this person through your group is a great start—so use it to get some more group time, or even one-on-one time, with your crush.

Finally, if your crush has just broken up with someone else in the group, of course you'll need to be sensitive to that. Still, it's imperative that everyone understand one thing clearly: Once two people have broken up, they have absolutely no say over who their ex dates next.

THE ALL-IMPORTANT "ASK"

There are two different ways of asking someone out on a date. The first is simply to indicate that you'd like to hang out: "We should get together sometime." This is a good lead-in for getting someone's number in order to call him or her up for a date—"Is it okay if I call you?" The second way to ask someone out is to do it directly: "Would you like to have dinner with me Friday night?"

When you call to ask someone out, always have a plan in mind, even if it's a spur-of-the-moment suggestion to go grab a bite. If it's someone you're really interested in, try to have a *real* invitation ready, including a specific activity (tailored to the other person's interests, if possible) and time frame.

The Good "Ask"

A good "ask" would go something like this:

> Tom: *"Hi, Elise. How's it going?"*
> Elise: *"I'm great. How 'bout you?"*
> Tom: *"I'm good, too. Listen, I was wondering if you'd like to go to dinner at that new Thai restaurant on Saturday. I know you've been wanting to try it ever since it opened."*

Regardless of whether Elise says yes or no, Tom has just executed a terrific ask. In two sentences, showing both consideration and confidence, he's suggested a date and a place and indicated that he had considered Elise's interests and tastes. Whether they're just friends or he's asking her out on a first date or they've been dating for some time, he did it right.

If the ask results in a "Yeah, sure," this is the time to establish where and when you're going to meet. Later, after Tom makes the dinner reservation (see Chapter 11, "Dining: A Night Out With Friends," page 140), he'll need to call Elise back and fill her in on other details, such as appropriate attire and whether he plans to take her to a movie or some other entertainment before or after dinner. (Tom can also send her the details by e-mail, but a phone call is more personal— and isn't that what dating is all about? Besides, with e-mail, if the other person doesn't check his or her in-box frequently, your message could go unread for some time.)

The Bad "Ask"

An "ask" that is too vague or open-ended comes across as a lack of confidence and consideration. Here's what *not* to do:

> Tom: *"Hey Elise, what's going on?"*
> Elise: *"Not much. And you?"*
> Tom: *"Oh, the usual. Umm, so, do you want to go to dinner or something sometime?"*
> Elise: *"Umm . . . sure."* (*It's such a vague offer, it's hard for her to respond with much enthusiasm.*)
> Tom: *"Great! Where do you want to go?"*
> Elise: *"I don't know. Where do you like to eat?"* (*She's surprised that he doesn't even have a place in mind—and so, being unsure herself, she throws the question back at him.*)
> Tom: *"Anything's good with me. What are you in the mood for?"*

Meanwhile, Elise is wondering how she's supposed to get excited about a rendezvous she hasn't actually been asked out on yet! It's been about two minutes now, and our boy still hasn't pinned down a date and time, let alone a place. By now, it's pretty obvious he hasn't thought of any agenda that would encourage Elise to want to go out to eat with him. In fact, he's basically put the ball in her court by expecting her to plan out their entire date.

THE DREADED ANSWERING MACHINE

uppose you call someone up to ask him or her out, and you get their answering machine or voice mail instead? Here's a great message to leave:

"Hey, Carrie, it's Jack. It's nine o'clock on Thursday. I hope you had a good day working in your studio. I was wondering if you were up for going out tonight. Or if you're busy, maybe we could go out some other time. Give me a call back. My number is 555-9034. Talk to you soon. Bye."

Anyone who gets a message like that will probably call back. Why? Because Jack did all the right things to make it easy for Carrie to respond. He . . .

- Left the time and day he called (this is really useful, since cell phone voice mail messages don't always come through right away)
- Wished her well and showed that he remembered what she did by asking about her day
- Clearly stated that he wanted to get together, and made a specific request (to go out tonight), while also offering an alternative if tonight wasn't convenient
- Left his number—*always* a good idea, since not everyone has caller ID—and
- Said a polite good-bye

SAYING NO

Elise could say either yes to Tom's good "ask" to dinner at the Thai restaurant—in which case, life for Tom is good—or she could say no. It's important to remember that *no* is not necessarily a bad thing. Elise might say no to this particular invitation, but there may be another night that works fine for her: "I'm afraid Friday isn't good for me. But next week is pretty open." Or she may say, "No, thank you, I'm afraid I'm busy that night," without mentioning any other possible times—an indication that she probably doesn't want to go to dinner with Tom at all.

If Tom sticks to his guns and proposes an alternative date but Elise doesn't want to pursue the matter, she can simply say, "Thanks for asking, but I just don't think this is going to work." That sends a clear message without being rude.

DATING 101: SMALL THINGS THAT MAKE A BIG DIFFERENCE

Here are some simple things we can do on dates that will leave the other person feeling relaxed and well-cared-for:

- *Be on time.* This shows that you are ready for the date, you're dependable, and you care enough about being with him or her to make the effort to be punctual.

- *Dress appropriately.* Bottom line—the atmosphere and your attire need to match. Consider whether this is a casual date or if you'll need to take your wardrobe up a notch. Your choice of dress sends serious signals about your social skills, not to mention your personality. A girl who wears a killer clubbing dress to a baseball game is clearly willing to embrace fashion at the risk of comfort. (It also indicates that she thinks clubbing attire belongs everywhere—which it doesn't.) A guy who wears jeans and a T-shirt to a nice restaurant is advertising that he doesn't know how to dress for a night out—or, even worse, that he knows but doesn't care enough to put in the effort.

- *Maintain your composure.* If you're driving to dinner or the movies and you're running late because of traffic, honking your horn and swearing will only make your date wonder what kind of a crazy you-know-what you are. And if you find it impossible to sit still or focus on your date because you're so concerned about when the food will arrive, she'll wonder whether you've gone out on the date for her or the appetizers. So chill out, relax, enjoy your date's company, and be aware of what signals your demeanor is sending.

- *Go easy on the alcohol.* There's nothing worse than suddenly realizing that your date is drunk. Tonight is not the night to test the limits of your tolerance. Period.

FLOWERS

Bringing your date a small bouquet to start your evening is simply a nice way to show that you appreciate the night you're about to have—whether it's with your significant other, someone you've just started dating, or even simply a good friend. And ladies: Don't get freaked out by a little old bouquet! All you have to do is thank your date and put the flowers in a vase. Here's another thought: The next time you're going over to his place, how about bringing *him* flowers? They'll spruce up his table, and he'll be pleasantly shocked.

THE BLIND DATE

Susanna's friend met a guy at a bar. Susanna's friend was already in a relationship, but she loves to play matchmaker, so she told the guy about Susanna. Then the friend told Susanna about the guy. Susanna agreed to let her friend pass along her phone number. His name was Aaron. He called two days later.

Blind date etiquette point 1: When arranging a blind date, the matchmaker must have everyone's consent before giving out anyone's phone number.

When Susanna and Aaron spoke on the phone, Aaron politely asked where Susanna might like to eat. She suggested meeting for some drinks and light appetizers at a restaurant bar she knows. That way, if they want to, they can go on to order dinner or at least linger over drinks. If, on the other hand, they just aren't feelin' each other, they can call it an early night without ruffling any feathers.

Blind date etiquette point 2: A get-together with a built-in time limit (translation: escape hatch) is a great idea for a blind date. Doing something light, like coffee, drinks, appetizers, or brunch, will allow you a good chance to get to know the other person without committing to a long, expensive dinner or night on the town.

The night before the date, Aaron called Susanna to confirm their plans. They agreed that he would pick her up at her place, and they'd walk to the restaurant from there.

Blind date etiquette point 3: Calling to confirm a blind date is especially considerate, since everyone's feeling a bit insecure to start with. And by the way, if you decide that you aren't going to make the rendezvous for some reason, you'd darned well better let the other person know. Pulling a no-show is just plain mean!

Since they'd already decided to go for drinks and appetizers, when Aaron and Susanna arrived at the restaurant, they chose to sit at a high table near the bar. They both ordered cocktails and picked two appetizers to share. Susanna found that Aaron certainly talked about himself a lot, but she assumed he was just nervous. Aaron thought Susanna certainly asked a lot of questions, but he figured that she was just trying to keep the conversation going. They laughed, they chatted, they certainly didn't cut the evening short—but when the time rolled around when they could have slipped over to the maitre d' and requested a table for dinner, they both realized they were perfectly content to leave it at appetizers and drinks. When he walked her home, both of them said they'd like to "do this again sometime" without really meaning it. They'd both had a good time but, in case you couldn't tell, there was *zero* chemistry between them.

That's the thing about blind dates—they're a completely mixed bag. Sometimes it takes another date or two for things to click. Sometimes the connection just isn't there from the start, and you know it. Or you meet someone who is cool, but for one reason or another, you don't see any possibility of a relationship coming out of it. The key to blind date etiquette is that both people go in knowing that rejection is possible and even okay, even though it's never fun.

Blind date etiquette point 4: *Above all, be honest: Don't say at the end of the evening that you'll call or that you'd really like to see the other person again, unless you mean it.*

Let's get back to Susanna and Aaron. Two days later, Aaron called Susanna again:

> *"Hi, Susanna."*
> *"Hey Aaron, how's it going?"*
> *"I was just calling to say that I really did have a good time on Thursday night, but I felt like there wasn't much chemistry between us. I sort of got the sense you felt that way, too."*

"Yeah, I kinda did. I'm sorry—I definitely had a good time, but, yeah, no spark."

"Okay, well, maybe we can hang out as friends sometime."

"Hey, you've got my number."

"Cool. So long, Susanna."

"Bye, Aaron. Thanks for calling."

I know what you're thinking: this exchange sounds scripted, as if I made it up to prove a point. But that is an actual, blow-by-blow description of what happened to my friend. She really didn't feel a spark, and she could tell that he didn't, either. My friend was especially grateful to him for his honesty. It made the whole experience stand out as a pleasant one, when it could have been lame or embarrassing. Now, *that's* etiquette.

THE DINNER DATE

For my parents' 30th wedding anniversary, my sister and I treated them to dinner for two at the restaurant where I had a summer job as a waitress. Although I wasn't working that night, I sneaked in for a drink, sitting in a darkened wait station where I could watch my parents enjoy their anniversary dinner.

What did I see? I saw my father hold my mother's chair for her as she sat down. I saw them making eye contact with each other as they talked. I saw Dad do his best not to "get distracted" by other diners. I watched as they offered each other samples from their respective plates. He poured her more wine, and she smiled warmly. No doubt about it—their intentions were clearly to make each other feel special, and they did.

ASK LIZZIE: LETTING YOUR DATE DOWN EASY

Q: What do you say at the end of a blind date—or *any* date—if you don't want to go out with the other person again?

LIZZIE: You're much better off being honest than saying something false or misleading. All too often we lie and tell the other person that "I'll call you," or that we had a great time and would like to see them again, because we want to appear likeable or don't want to hurt them. But all you really need to do is indicate that you had a nice time, say good-bye, and *leave it at that:* "I really enjoyed dinner. Thanks so much. Good night!" Lie, and you only bring yourself and the other person down.

If the other person asks you to go out again, you'll need to be more straightforward. It takes a lot of courage and honesty, but you know in your gut that you're better off for saying it: "Jen, I'm sorry, but I just don't think this is going to work." If the other person starts acting insulted, defensive, or hurt, you just have to realize that those feelings will fade—and that while they may be bummed now, they'll get over it a lot faster than if you'd led them on.

When it's just the two of you dining out, whether it's a first date or you're celebrating an important occasion or a milestone such as an anniversary, you are obviously making an effort to spend quality time with someone who is special or potentially special to you. This is a time when every move counts:

- If you're the one choosing the restaurant, be sure to ask about your companion's food preferences: You don't want to take a vegetarian to a steakhouse!

- If you're going to be picking up the check, you may want to call the restaurant ahead of time to find out the price range.

- If you're planning to go straight from dinner to a movie, play, or concert, let the restaurant know at the time you're making the reservation. The staff can help make sure you're leaving enough time to get to your event.

SMOOTH OPERATOR

As for all you guys out there, maybe you're used to holding doors and chairs for women, and maybe not. But if a dinner date doesn't call for your best manners, what does? The following gestures, when handled confidently and with communication, will show that you know how to pull out all the stops, without seeming over the top.

Hold the Door for Her

Holding the door for a date is such a simple move, and it truly has a lot of class. As the couple approaches the restaurant door (or any other door), the man steps forward slightly and pulls or pushes open the door, allowing the woman to walk through first. And if there is a second door? Don't panic—either she'll open it herself or wait for the man to open it for her. Whatever the situation, the man should never rush. Opening a door for someone—whether it be a man or a woman—should always be a smooth, relaxed act of kindness and consideration.

WHEN IN DOUBT, ASK

I f you're worried about what your date would prefer in a given situation, ask before you act:

- "Can I hold your coat for you?"
- "Would you like a drink or just some wine?"
- "Can I get your chair for you?"
- "Ooh, that entrée sounds good; when the waiter comes over, would you like me to order for you?"
- "Do you want to wait here while I go get the car?"

Help Her Off With Her Coat

Helping a date off with her coat is one gesture that should *always* be done. Hold the shoulders of her coat as she takes it off and help her slide it off her arms. Then hang both coats up, or carry them to the coat check. After dinner, do the reverse—hold your date's coat open for her and gently slip it onto her shoulders as she slides her arms in. And don't forget to tip the coat check attendant. (See "Tipping 101," page 218.)

Hold Her Chair for Her

Holding your date's chair and making sure that she's seated comfortably at the table is one of those traditional gestures that's thought of as old-fashioned nowadays. Old-fashioned or not, it's still a lovely, considerate move, and I find myself surprisingly touched whenever someone does it for me. Some guys avoid doing it simply because they aren't sure the gesture will be appreciated. Here's a simple solution: Before you reach for the back of her chair, turn to your date and say, "Would you like me to hold your chair for you?" Now it's her choice to say, "Why yes, please" or, "No, thank you." Either way, confusion and awkwardness are avoided, and consideration shines through.

MAKING CONVERSATION

The objective of going out to dinner is to eat good food, soak up the atmosphere, and have pleasant conversation with your date for the evening. So what do you talk about?

If you're on a first date, you have about eighty-four thousand questions to choose from. Where are you from? What do you do? How did you end up in this city? What do you do outside of work? Where did you go to college? Where have you traveled? It's almost a paralyzingly huge list when you really think about it. A hilarious TV show once portrayed a girl trying to get to know a cute guy next door. She spent every second they had together listing things she liked, trying to get him to talk. Finally someone standing near them whispered to her: "Try asking him about what he likes." So she asked what type of music he listens to, and he turned and started a lively conversation. It's that simple.

When you're out on a date, no matter how long you've known the other person, give him or her a chance to talk about what they know. You don't have to get personal, but you do have to make an effort to listen and respond—it's called conversation! The reason you're dining together in the first place is likely because you enjoy one another's company. So let your date know it by showing interest in his or her life. (For a discussion of appropriate conversation topics, see "What Should We Talk About?" page 153.)

WHO PAYS?

The other week, a friend treated me to breakfast because I'd paid for her drinks the week before. When we got to the restaurant I still wasn't sure she was actually going to pay. (I don't ever want to assume I'm being taken care of when I'm not—which is why I always keep my wallet on me.) But as we got out of the car, Amy said, "Now remember, I'm treating you for taking care of me the other night." It was a relief to know for sure what was going on. When the bill came, I didn't even look at it. I just let her handle it and thanked her for a great breakfast out.

When it comes to paying the bill on a date, there is one rule of thumb to follow: Unless you discussed a different arrangement when you set up the date, *whoever did the inviting should do the paying.* Above all, there should be no surprises: You should never get to the end of the meal and find out that you're expected to split the bill, when the assumption all along was that it would be taken care of by the person who invited you.

There are times, of course, when it may be preferable for each person to pay for his or her own meal. Again, this should be made clear at the time the dinner invitation is extended. A friend of mine recently went on a quasi-date: Her friend's brother wanted to take her to lunch and she agreed, but she made it clear from the get-go that she

INSTANT TIP

If you're taking someone out and you're planning to pick up the tab, gently reassure him or her at the very start of the evening that you're paying: "Don't forget, this is on me!" That way, you can both relax and have a great time.

wasn't comfortable being "taken out." So they made an agreement up front to split the bill: "Lunch sounds great—how about going Dutch?"

If someone invites you to an event and you'd like to return the favor, you could offer to pay for some other part of the evening: "I'd love to go to the concert with you. Can I treat you to dinner before?"

"THANK YOU!"

When the dinner date is over, regardless of whether or not you want to go out with this particular person again, both of you should be sure to thank the other for a nice evening together.

If you had a great time and you do want to see the other person again, let him or her know with a phone call the following day. It's perfectly fine to leave a voice mail message (or send an e-mail, for that matter): "Hey, Andy, I just wanted to say thanks again for a great time last night. That restaurant was fabulous. Hope to see you soon. Bye!"

Better yet, if you *really* want to make a statement, write your date an actual thank-you note. How great is it to come home two or three days after a date and find a handwritten note waiting for you, reminding you of the great time you had? I know that I'd be both surprised and *very* pleased. And who knows? If the date leads to something big, you've got a real keepsake to hang onto and cherish.

CHAPTER 15

LET THE GAMES BEGIN!

THE ETIQUETTE OF SPORTS AND FITNESS

WHAM! GRUNT, RUN, run, run, and turn . . . *Wham!* Right down the line, slide, reach up . . . *Smash!* Game point. The energy, the power, the ferocity, the utter high (for me) obtained from a great tennis match is such an awesome, powerful, feeling: "I am Lizzie, ultimate ruler of the tennis court! With my racket in hand, I am to be feared!"

Well, maybe not literally—but hey, whether we're striving against ourselves, another person, or a whole team, sports uplift us. The endorphins race, the sweat pours, the muscles ache, but who cares—you're on top of your game!

You gotta love it. Just be careful that you don't love it *too* much: No matter how into a sport or exercise activity you may be, you still have to think about how the actions you take affect those around you, both on and off the field. It doesn't matter if you're involved in a quick pickup game at the gym or a college varsity match or a corporate team championship: As a competitor, how you conduct yourself matters.

ETIQUETTE ON THE ATHLETIC FIELD

As an athlete, your conduct will depend partly on the type of sports activity you're involved in. Here are some tips on the most common scenarios:

Pickup Games

When you play on a team, you and your teammates have a certain rapport. You know your mates' pressure points, you know how to move with them, you know who's a ball hog and who will always find you when you're open—the point is, you *know*. During pickup games, on the other hand, you *don't* always know, either about your opponents or your own teammates. That six-foot-five, 220-lb. center might get really P.O.'d when you steal the ball from him, or the other players might see you as a drag on the field because they play on the varsity team. With that in mind, here are a few things you can do to make pickup games go more smoothly:

THE GRACEFUL WINNER (AND LOSER)

Perhaps things got a little heated out there on the court—but in the end it's just a game, right? The considerate player downplays his or her victories ("Good match! For a while there, I thought you had me") and is generous in defeat ("Nice win! Your serve was awesome today").

- **Introduce yourself.** At the start of the game, shake hands with the other players and tell them your name. Not only is this a polite gesture but when you're playing, it's a lot easier to say, "Yo, Trev, I'm open!" than to yell, "Hey you!" to a court full of players.

- **Tread lightly.** If you have a tendency to "direct" play while you're on the field, a pickup game is not the time to indulge it. While this kind of leadership can be helpful and welcome once you've established credibility with your teammates, in a pickup game it may be taken as overstepping or even arrogance.

- **Try to avoid arguing over calls.** Since you typically don't know the players in a pickup game as well as you know your friends or teammates, you're also going to want to avoid challenging the other team's calls if at all possible. There usually aren't referees for these games, which leaves players to call their own fouls and penalties. This can be a point of friction in any game—but when playing with people you don't know, aggressively challenging another player's call can easily escalate into a full-scale argument. If you do decide to question a ruling, be careful what words you use; you never know how a stranger will receive them.

Regular or Team Games

When playing in a regular group—in a weekly volleyball game for instance, or on an organized team—you have the advantage of knowing the other players. Even among close friends, however, a couple of key etiquette points are worth remembering:

- **Always be on time.** Often, tennis courts, tee times, and field reservations are difficult to come by, which is why athletic facilities usually run on tight schedules. If you have a small group that plays tennis together every week and you only have the court for an hour and a half, imagine how you would feel if one guy continually showed up thirty minutes late. We all treasure our time away from work and school, and no one wants to spend that precious time waiting. It's especially important to be on time if you're the member of a team. Coaches don't want players who don't respect the team's time, because they simply can't function if the whole team is held up waiting for one player.

- *Never take your fellow players for granted.* A good experience depends on the support of your entire group, not just the best players. So don't ignore someone or write them off because they might be one of the group's weaker links. Instead, cheer everyone's efforts, even your opponents'. Remember: You're *all* there to play the game and have a good time in the process.

Whenever You Play

Whether you play on a team, in a regular group, or in pickup games, the following points of sportsmanship apply everywhere:

- *Don't let winning become worthless.* It's okay to want to win, but when winning becomes so important that it devalues the victory itself, you know you have a problem. When we start calling shots out that were really in, kicking the ball a little to improve our lie, or sneaking in some cheap moves—checking, elbowing, tripping—to score a goal or gain control of the ball, then we're undermining the very competitive values that are supposedly driving us. If you feel you have to use unsportsman-like conduct for the sake of winning, it's a shame—and the win has become worthless.

- ***Don't carry the competition off the field.*** My boyfriend plays in a soccer league, and recently his team had a game against a serious rival. The game was fairly heated, and afterward one of his teammates decided to let off some steam. Rather than grabbing a few beers with the rest of the guys or going for a hard run, he got in his car, peeled out of the gravel parking lot, and sprayed the other team's cars with rocks—all while giving them the finger. Trevor was pretty mad that his teammate reacted this way. They had an important match against the same team the next week, and a win would have taken them to finals. Instead, the other team was fired up from the stunt the week before, and pulled off a victory in overtime.

By continuing the competition off the field, you cause a number of problems for yourself. First of all, you invite trouble. Any one of the opposing team's members could just as easily pursue you off the field and out of the public eye. There are also your teammates to consider: You're not alone out there—you're part of a team, and your behavior reflects on everyone else. In fact, your teammates may decide they don't want a player who can't handle herself off the field. Plus, some leagues really frown upon this kind of behavior, and you may be expelled because of it. So when it comes to anger on the field, leave it there or, better yet, let it go completely.

THE CONSIDERATE FAN

Let's just say that we fans can all get a little crazy. I grew up going religiously to the University of Vermont Catamounts' men's hockey games (I attended my first game three weeks after I was born). I loved the yelling, I loved the rare goals we scored, and I loved my section,

CHEER, DON'T JEER

My tennis coach had one major rule when it came to cheering for our teammates on the court. He said, "Only cheer when we win a point because of a well-placed shot. Don't cheer because the other girl messed up." We all want our team to win. That's fine. But when cheering turns into jeering, we've let the game get to us.

section 21. We were a tight-knit group who loved our Cats—sometimes a little too much.

I remember being ten years old and going to one of the usual Friday-night games. One of things I loved about hockey games was that I could yell and scream and cheer to my heart's content, knowing that my little voice would be drowned out by everyone in the crowd. Until the night that it wasn't. It happened that a big ol' nasty player on the other team came into the penalty box (conveniently located directly below our seats). Everyone was jeering him, yet somehow out of that jeering one pipsqueak's voice could be heard, loud and clear: "Take a seat, you f***ing asshole!"

My dad turned and looked at me in shock. I could feel that awful feeling, when you know you just overstepped the boundaries, not by a little but by a lot. "Lizzie!" he exclaimed, and he gave me that look—the one that's sort of questioning, sort of disappointed, definitely reproachful, and a little curious as to what you are going to say next. That night, I learned my lesson about what it means to cheer appropriately.

Of course, proper fan etiquette varies widely by sport. At a basketball game, it's mandatory whenever a player is shooting a foul shot for the fans of the opposing team to cause as much distraction as humanly possible. But less rowdy sports such as tennis or golf expect

THE GUY BEHIND YOU

D on't you just hate it when the guy behind you keeps spilling popcorn on you, talks throughout the game, or insists on using those oh-so-annoying blow-up sticks that you smack together to make an ungodly amount of noise (and which I have a personal vendetta against)?

Here's what to do: If the person's actions have bothered you more than once, turn around and say, very softly and politely, "Excuse me, but would you mind holding your popcorn a little tighter? It seems to be relocating to my shirt. Thank you." If he doesn't respond to a polite request or, worse, reacts belligerently, don't pursue things any further yourself. Instead, find an usher and explain the situation. It's the responsibility of stadium personnel to keep an eye on the offending fan, and to step in or even remove him if he continues to be a problem.

their fans to meet a different standard. While there's a lot more shouting and cheering between points in these sports than there used to be, one rule still holds: When the point is being played, you should never yell at the players or disturb them by moving around. Hold your tongue and stay in your seat until the play is over—then you can cheer or jump all you want!

RESPECT THE REF

We also have to watch ourselves when it comes to bashing the refs. One battle does not win a war, and one bad play or call does not lose the game. Referees have a tough job. A baseball umpire, for example, makes around 150 calls each game. If he makes 3 calls that are questionable, he gets ripped apart by the fans, even though 3 out of 150 gives him a 98 percent success rate. If you still can't see where I'm coming from, invite ten of your friends to come to your office and start jeering at you when you make a mistake—or when they *think* you did. Then you'd get a small taste of how it feels to be a referee.

HEALTH CLUB ETIQUETTE

Exercising at a health club isn't supposed to be competitive, but it sure can seem that way when you and three other people are going for the same elliptical trainer. Whenever you've got a lot of sweaty people doing a lot of energetic things on the same pieces of equipment, etiquette becomes essential: With it, everyone does what they need to do with minimum wait or fuss. Without it, you've got disrupted workouts and disgruntled exercisers.

Here are ten etiquette points to keep in mind the next time you're at the gym:

1. First and foremost, *always* wipe your sweat off all equipment after using it. This goes for mats as well as machines.

2. *No cutting!* If someone else is next in line to use a machine, it's theirs—no questions asked.

3. Don't hog the weight machines. If the gym is crowded, try rotating your sets instead of focusing on one machine at a time.

4. Always reset the weight machines after you're done with them. This way, they can be easily set by the next person.

5. Don't overstay your time on the cardio machines. Many gyms either limit the number of minutes that you can stay on a given machine or have people schedule their session in advance. If someone is waiting for your machine, let them know how much longer you expect to be.

6. Respect other people's sign-up times. If you begin your treadmill session five minutes later than your scheduled time, that means you get five fewer minutes on your cardio session; extend your time past that, and you'll make the next user late as well.

7. Abide by the rules of your fitness center. These are some common ones to look for: turn off all cell phones; always sign in; eat only in designated areas; and wear proper shoes.

8. Avoid putting on perfume or cologne before you work out; the sweat emphasizes the aromas and the result may be more than some other members can stand.

9. Be on time for personal training sessions and group classes.

10. Do your part to help keep the locker room clean: don't leave your hair in the shower drain; use a paper towel to wipe down the sink after using it; and make sure your towels make it into the laundry bin.

CHAPTER 16

DRIVER'S ED-IQUETTE

W E ALL KNOW that leaning on your horn out of anger, scream-ing at or taunting another driver, or flashing a rude ges-ture (you know the one I mean) are all forms of road rage, not to mention (need I say it?) *major* etiquette vio-lations, and should be kept in check at all times. But there are also some simpler things that we can do to keep our driver's ed-iquette on the up and up.

USE YOUR BLINKER

Letting someone know well ahead of time that you're planning to turn or switch lanes helps them to be prepared. Using your blinker, or turn signal, is far more considerate than forcing the driver behind you to slam on the brakes—plus you're risking a rear-end collision if they can't slow down quickly enough.

The same thing holds for turning off your blinker. Once you've switched lanes or made a turn, it's important to turn your blinker off,

HEADS UP: THE DIFFERENCE BETWEEN A HELPFUL PASSENGER AND A PAIN IN THE BUTT

When you're a passenger in a car and you indicate something to look out for in the road, such as a car that's pulling out of a driveway or side street or suddenly changing lanes, you're being helpful. When you comment on someone's driving, however: "Why did you turn your blinker on so early?" or, "You so could have passed him back there," or, "If you'd taken Dorset we'd be there now," you're being a pain in the butt. Before you make a comment to the driver, consider whether your comment will truly be helpful—or whether you're butting in unnecessarily.

---

if it hasn't automatically done so. Otherwise, you're literally sending false signals to the drivers around you.

THE HORN HAS MANY VOICES

Your vehicle's horn is an important warning device that is there to be used. The secret is to use it in the right way:

- A succession of short, light beeps lets someone know you're saying hi.

- A quick little beep gives another driver a quick heads-up that you're there.

- A slightly louder, slightly longer beep conveys a more assertive message: *Hey, the light's been green for ten seconds!* or, *Yo, watch it!*

- A longer blast from the horn, repeated several times, is usually an impatient driver: *Come* on, *let's go!*

- A long, unremitting blast obviously is saying, *I'm P.O.'d and I'm letting you and everyone in the world know it—which also shows that I've lost control.*

When you start taking your frustration out by using your horn, it's a sign that you've crossed a line. To cure horn-itis, make a conscious effort to use your horn the right way—to let someone know what's happening on the road—and learn to exercise a little patience.

GOING OVER THE LIMIT

Beeping your horn at a driver who is too close is one thing, but deliberately belligerent behavior—like giving another driver the finger, leaning on the horn as hard as you can, or intentionally tailgating someone or cutting them off—is not only bad driving etiquette but also potentially dangerous. Remember, you don't have the slightest idea who that person in the other car is; if he or she is prone to road rage, you could be running a serious personal risk by indulging in this sort of provocative behavior.

BE CONSIDERATE OF YOUR PASSENGERS

Not all of us can handle being driven around by a Mario Andretti, and even fewer of us want to. It can be nerve-wracking to be a passenger in a car that's being driven too fast: You're not the one at the wheel, and all control over your fate is in the hands of an inconsiderate (and dangerous) driver. So drivers, when you do have passengers, be aware of their comfort levels. Slow the speed down a little, take the turns a bit easier, and in general be more considerate in everything you do. Your passengers will feel safe and confident in your driving skills, and you'll be a better driver for it.

CHAPTER 17

FOUR TIMES WHEN YOU'VE GOT TO GET IT RIGHT

HERE ARE CERTAIN MOMENTS when etiquette is more than just helpful, it's essential. Two of the situations discussed in this chapter—leaving a tip after a good meal and writing to thank your Aunt Millicent for a birthday gift—may seem a little mundane at first glance. The others involve two of life's major milestones, when you're invited to a wedding and you have to express your sympathy for someone's loss. But all four situations have one thing in common: They're all moments of heightened interaction between people. When you're living on your own, you'll encounter every one of these situations at some point. And I'm sure you'd rather get it right—so read on.

TIPPING 101

Whether he's signing the check at a restaurant or slipping the valet or door attendant a few bills, our friend Suave always knows how to do the tipping thing subtly and smoothly, without ever making a show of it. Want to be that guy? The following section will tell you exactly how much—and how—to tip for some common services.

Restaurant Waiters

For acceptable service from a waiter, the minimum standard tip across the United States is 15 percent of the bill *before* tax has been added to it. In major cities, 15 to 20 percent is standard. You can write in the tip on your bill, if paying by credit or debit card, or leave it as cash (placed inside the book that the bill came in or directly on the table). Before leaving a tip, though, check to make sure an automatic service charge (usually 15 or 18 percent) hasn't already been added to your bill. If it has, you aren't obligated to tip anything more (although you can always add an additional tip if you think the waiter deserves it).

Bartenders

The standard tip for a bartender is 10 to 15 percent of whatever you spend on alcohol. If you're paying as you go, you should ideally leave a tip each time you buy a drink, usually put down in bills (never less than a dollar) on the bar. If you're running a tab, leave your tip when you settle up. (Add a couple of extra dollars if the bartender gave you free drinks.) If you're having drinks while waiting for your table and your drink tab will be added to your dinner bill, leave a separate cash tip for the bartender as you leave the bar.

Washroom Attendants

Tip 50 cents if a washroom attendant simply hands you a paper towel. If he brushes off your jacket or she does a quick mend to the hem of your dress, give the attendant $2 or $3. The tip is usually placed in a small dish, rather than handed to the attendant. If the attendant does nothing, there's no need for you to tip.

Coat-Check Attendants

Tip the coat-check attendant $2 for the first coat and $1 for each additional coat. When you collect your coats, give the tip directly to the attendant or place it in the waiting dish, if there is one.

Parking Valets

Tip a parking valet $2 in smaller cities and $3 to $4 in larger cities. Hand the parking attendant the cash tip after he brings your car to you—not when you arrive.

Airport Skycaps and Curbside Baggage Checkers

Tip a skycap or baggage checker $1 to $2 per bag—and $3 or more if a bag is very heavy—handed to him in cash after the bags have been delivered to their destination.

Taxi Drivers

The tip for a taxi ride is usually about 20 percent of the fare, but for very short rides you should tip a minimum of $1. If the driver helps you with suitcases or packages, you may want to tip a little more (50 cents per bag is standard). If you use a car service, check with the driver to see whether a tip is included automatically in the fee. If so, there's no need for you to add anything.

At a Hotel

The **door attendant** is tipped not for opening the door but for other small tasks: $1 to $4 if he hails a cab for you (add $1 if it's raining), requests your car from the garage, or loads your bags into your car. The **bellhop** should be tipped $1 per bag, and never less than $2 total (if he's especially helpful, add $1 or $2 more). The **hotel concierge** is usually tipped $5 to $10 for each service she performs, such as recommending a restaurant and making a reservation for you; for performance above and beyond, such as getting tickets to a nearly sold out concert, tip $15. The tip for **room service waiters** is often included in the bill, so check carefully for this. If there's no service charge included, tip 15 to 20 percent of the bill, and never less than $2. At the end of your stay, tip the **housekeeping staff** $3 to $5 per person for each night in a luxury hotel, and $2 per person per night in a less-expensive hotel. You can leave the tip in cash on the bureau of your room (with a brief thank-you note, so they know that you didn't accidentally leave the money behind), or you can put it in a sealed envelope marked "Housekeeper" with your name and room number, and leave it at the front desk.

At a Beauty Salon

If several people have worked on you, tip each person separately at the end of your visit, based on the totals for the individual services as listed on your bill. **Hairdressers**, **colorists**, and **manicurists** typically get a tip of 15 to 20 percent. If a separate person gives you a shampoo, tip him or her $2 to $3.

Building Staff

If you live in an apartment building, it's customary to tip the building staff at the holidays. Give $20 to $80 to a live-in **superintendent** (the more luxurious your building, the higher the tip is expected to be), $35 to $80 to the most helpful **door attendant** and other staff, and $20 to $30 to employees you rarely see.

Garage Attendants

Whether you've parked overnight or you leave your car in the garage for a few hours while shopping or doing errands, hand the attendant $1 to $2 when he brings your car to you.

Delivery People

Anyone delivering restaurant takeout food to your door should be tipped somewhere between 10 and 20 percent of the (pretax) cost of the food. (For orders of only a few dollars, tip a little higher.) However, you are *not* obligated to tip people who deliver furniture, large appliances, or similar items.

Writing a Thank-You Note

Sending someone a handwritten thank-you note is a real sign of appreciation—especially in today's technology-driven world of e-mails and instant messaging. A handwritten note speaks volumes: It shows that you took the time to sit down and spell out your appreciation for this person. Showing that we appreciate what others do for us is an act of consideration, pure and simple, as was the favor, gift, or hospitality of the person we are now thanking.

While it's best to send a thank-you note within a week of receiving the gift or the favor, you should never *not* send one. Even if it's a year late, send the note. Believe me, it will make the other person feel wonderful to receive it.

What should you write? Write exactly what you would say if the other person were right there with you. For example:

> *Dear Angelo and Marylene,*
> *I was so happy you could attend my graduation ceremony and celebration. It meant so much to me to have you there.*

You've supported me throughout high school and college and have taught me so much. I also want to thank you for the gorgeous opal necklace and the silver hair clip. I actually don't own any opal (which is my birthstone), and the hair clip is the only one that holds all of my hair. They are both very thoughtful gifts.

Thank you again.

Much love,
Lizzie

Or, if you're writing to someone you're not as close with:

Dear Ted and Becky,

I really appreciated your letting me stay with you during my visit to see Harvard. You have a lovely home, and you made me feel very welcome in it. I hope you enjoy the flowers—I remember Becky saying that dahlias are her favorite.

Again, thank you for sharing your home with me. I hope to see you both again in the future.

Sincerely,
Lizzie

You want to acknowledge what the recipient has done for you, then write a sentence or two about the gift or your stay. There's a big difference between sending a note that says "Thanks for the flowers" and one that says, "Thank you for the flowers—they truly brighten the front hall as I walk in the house." Adding a line or two about how much you appreciate the gift, what you'll use it for, or how much you enjoyed your stay makes the note more personal.

YOU'RE INVITED TO
A WEDDING

This wedding stuff is a pretty big deal. Two people decide they want to spend the rest of their lives loving one another, and they want *you* to be a part of their celebration of it. Whether you're the maid of honor, a cousin of the groom, or attending as your boyfriend's guest, you've been invited to a wedding. So what do you do now?

The first thing you might receive is a save-the-date card. With this card, the bride and groom are asking you to keep the date of their wedding open and mark it on your calendar so you don't forget. The reasons for a save-the-date card? Maybe it's early in the game, and the wedding invitations aren't ready yet. Or the wedding might require advance travel planning on your part. You don't need to send a response: Just make sure you (one more time for the people in the back!) *save the date*.

The Wedding Invitation

The actual invitation will arrive about six to eight weeks before the wedding. It contains the following vital information:

- **Who's "giving the wedding"**: The bride's family, for example, or the bride and groom themselves

- **Who's getting married**: The names of the bride and groom

- **When they're getting married**: The date and time of the big event

- **Where they're getting married**: The name and location of both the ceremony and the reception

- **Who you can bring, if anyone:** The invitation will be addressed in one of three ways: either to you alone, to you and your significant other, or to you "and Guest"

- **Where to RSVP:** Wedding invitations typically include a *response card*, along with a stamped, preaddressed envelope. Your card will look something like this:

M_____
ACCEPTS_____
REGRETS_____
PLEASE SEND YOUR RESPONSE BY JUNE 12TH

You may also see a selection of dinners to choose from. The card might indicate a choice of filet mignon or salmon, for instance, in which case you'll put a check mark next to the entrée you prefer.

Some invitations simply include a name and address to which you'll write your own response on a sheet of stationery. (If no RSVP address is listed, send your RVSP to the return address on the invitation.) For a formal affair, your response should be in the third person and mirror the style of the invitation itself:

Miss Tanya Jones
accepts with pleasure
[or *"regrets that she is unable to accept"*—*if she can't go*]
the invitation of
Mr. and Mrs. Mark Furla
to the marriage of their daughter
Katherine Marie
to
Mr. Reeve Smith
Saturday, the second of May

Note: If "and guest" has been indicated (and you're bringing one), you may list either:

Miss Tanya Jones and Guest

or

Miss Tanya Jones and Mr. John Bartly

If the wedding is less formal or you know the hosts well, you can write a brief personal note in the first person:

Dear Mr. and Mrs. Furla,

John and I are delighted to accept your invitation to Katie and Reeve's wedding on May second. We look forward to seeing you there!

Love,
Tanya

All About Invitations

- **When do I send a response?** Send your response immediately, or as soon as you know whether you can attend. You don't want the bride to have to call and inquire whether you're coming.

INSTANT TIP

If you've been invited to an engagement party, you are *not* required to bring a gift. Those who do give gifts to congratulate the couple on their engagement are usually close friends and family members, and they will send or present their gifts privately.

- *If I accept the invitation, does this mean I have to give the bride and groom a wedding gift?* Yes, always. Don't worry if your budget is tight—you're not expected to break the bank for a wedding gift. In most instances, the bridal registry should have items in a range of prices. (See box, "The Gift Registry," page 228.) You can send the gift anytime after you receive the invitation.

- *If I send my regrets that I won't be attending, do I still have to give a gift?* Yes, almost always. Being invited to a wedding is the one time when you are always required to send a gift, even if you turn down the invitation. (The only exception is if you're an extremely casual acquaintance who somehow got invited and you don't plan on attending.) Why, you may ask, are you required to send a gift if you're not going to the wedding? Because the person getting married thinks enough of you to want you there to witness his or her vows—and that's a big deal.

- *May I bring a guest?* Only if your invitation specifies that you're allowed to bring a guest. If the words "and Guest" do not appear anywhere on your invitation, you may *not* show up with a guest in tow—*nor may you ask* if you can bring a guest. Calling to wheedle an extra slot will only put your hosts on the spot. Cheer up, though. While you may feel a little lonely attending a wedding without a date, this day isn't about you—it's about the couple getting married. You should feel honored and happy that they have requested your presence, even if you wind up dancing with the twelve-year-old ring bearer.

There's actually a very practical reason for the "no surprise guests" rule: Weddings are very expensive events, and caterers usually base their prices on head counts. Your hosts have decided that they are able to accommodate only you, without a guest, and you need to respect that decision. Showing up with an uninvited

THE GIFT REGISTRY

A wedding gift registry is designed to help guests know what the couple already has (or what other guests have already purchased) and what they still need. It ensures that the newlyweds don't wind up with five gravy boats, one tea set, no saucers, and only four spoons. Either the mother of the bride or the maid of honor is usually responsible for letting guests know about the registry. (It's rare that you'll ever be asked to contact the bride directly for her registry information.) Once you've received your invitation, get in touch with the mother of the bride or the maid of honor, who will have a list of stores or Web sites where the bride is registered, and how to access them.

When you do, you're likely to find a wide selection of registry gifts to choose from. Traditionally, wedding gifts were little offerings to help the newlyweds set up their first home. More often than not, gifts are still centered around the home; however, there are some who push the limits (I know of one bride who put cosmetic surgery on her registry list! Ridiculous!). Know that just because a bride and groom are registered, you don't have to buy a gift on their list. It's absolutely fine to give them any present you like and can afford.

---

guest throws everything off, from seating to food (especially if the reception is a sit-down dinner). If you're single and on your own, hold your head up and go as your fabulous self. Besides, you never know what cute bridesmaid, groomsman, usher, or other guest is hoping that a single like you will be there.

What to Wear to a Wedding

GUEST	FORMAL DAY	FORMAL EVENING	SEMIFOR-MAL DAY	SEMIFOR-MAL EVENING	INFORMAL DAY	INFORMAL EVENING
Female	Full-length cocktail or summer dress	Full-length or short cocktail or formal dress	Short or long dress, skirt and top com-bination, or dressy pantsuit	Short or long cock-tail dress or skirt and top combi-nation	Skirt and top com-bination, pantsuit, or sundress	Cocktail dress of any length
Male	Dark suit, conserva-tive tie and shoes	Tuxedo if specified; dark suit otherwise	Dark suit	Dark suit	Dark suit, or light trousers and dark blazer in the summer	Dark suit

Wedding Attire

The last bit of information the invitation will contain is how you should dress for the occasion. Here's where things can get a little tricky. If the invitation states "Black Tie," you're wearing a tux. If it states "Black Tie Preferred," or "Black Tie Optional," it's up to you to determine what you're going to wear, based on the time and formality of the wedding. The chart on the preceding page will help you out.

At the Reception

At the entrance to the reception, you're very likely to see a receiving line consisting of the wedding party and the bride's and groom's parents. Be patient and wait your turn to go through it (no making a beeline for the bar). When your turn arrives, congratulate the people you know and introduce yourself to those you don't, being sure to mention your connection to the wedding ("Hi, I'm Mike. I went to college with the groom").

Once at the reception, your task is easy: Enjoy yourself and the company of the other guests. This is also a perfect opportunity to put all of your etiquette skills into play. Remember your conversation do's (see "Dinner Conversation," page 151), as well as your icebreakers (see

INSTANT TIP

Serving alcohol at a wedding is fairly standard, and a lot of receptions feature an open bar. This doesn't mean you have a green light to drink yourself under the table, however. Think how disappointed you would be if someone got tanked on *your* special day. This is a time to know your limits and stick to them.

~ ASK LIZZIE: NO SWITCHING! ~

Q: I was at a friend's wedding recently and discovered that a bunch of other close friends were sitting at a different table than I was. I was tempted to switch place cards so that my date and I could sit at their table, but my date talked me out of it. Was he right?

LIZZIE: Your date was completely correct in stopping you. If the reception includes a seated meal with place cards, this usually means that great care has gone into planning the seating. You need to respect your host's plan—which means no switching cards or asking anyone to change places with you. Once the main course is finished and dessert is being served, however, it's usually acceptable to leave your seat and migrate around the room.

"Find a Way to Break the Ice," page 178), and, of course, your knowledge of table manners (see Chapter 12, "Dining: The Mechanics of It All," page 158). If it's a sit-down dinner, be sure to spend time talking to those seated with you.

Finally, when you've danced the night away and it's time to go home, be sure to thank both the bride's and the groom's parents, as well as the happy couple themselves. It was a great party, and they should know how much you appreciated being a part of it all.

The Thank-You Note

Having selected the perfect gift and settled on the perfect outfit, you show up at the wedding (with or without a date) and have a fantastic time. The happy couple has been wed and celebrated, and everyone has gone home, tired and happy. Now it's time to write your hosts a thank-you note for throwing such an amazing party.

Dear Mr. And Mrs. Furla,

Thank you so much for throwing such a wonderful wedding. The setting was enchanting, and the day was truly a perfect celebration of Katie and Reeve's feelings for each other. I was thrilled and touched to have been a part of witnessing their declaration of love. All of the best to both of you and the happy couple as they start their life together.

Many thanks,
Tanya Jones

WHEN A DEATH OCCURS

Sadly, we are faced with funerals and the loss of loved ones throughout our lives. As a newly independent, one aspect of growing up that's easy to overlook is the etiquette surrounding death. What do you do when a friend's father dies or a member of your own family passes away? Some people become wonderful sources for comfort and compassion, while others shut down and don't know what to do or say in the face of such tragedy.

As a friend of someone who is grieving, even if you aren't certain what to do or say, don't worry that your efforts to comfort or get in touch are an intrusion in a sorrowful time. While your friend may be confused and hurting, your friendship is undoubtedly welcome.

Sending Flowers

When sending flowers, truly any bouquet or potted plant will show you care. Flowers may be sent either to the funeral home or to the deceased's family. While any time is an appropriate time to send flowers, the closer they're sent to when you were told the news, the better.

Observing Visiting Hours

Before you decide to go console your friend and pay your respects to the deceased, check the visiting hours of the funeral home or the hours that the family has indicated. (They should be included in the death notice in the newspaper.) When you go to visit, you should pay your respects to the deceased either by saying a little prayer over the coffin or urn or by pausing by it for a moment of reflection. Then proceed to the family to offer your sympathy. You'll also want to sign the guest register. This is so that the family can thank all those who came to pay their respects.

At the Service

Now is really a time to pull it together and be respectful. During the service, the only thing you should excuse yourself for is if you have a persistent cough or you're caring for a crying child. Otherwise, you should remain seated and still during the service. Remember, too, to double-check that your cell phone is turned *off*.

WHAT TO OFFER A GRIEVING FRIEND

- Child care services
- A prepared meal
- Help with notifications
- Help with cleaning the house
- Flowers
- Help with keeping a record of flowers and offerings sent to the family
- To go for a walk together
- To bring over a good movie
- A listening ear
- A hug

WHAT TO SAY—AND WHAT *NOT* TO SAY

I f you're like a lot of people, you may be uncertain about what you should say to a grieving family member. You'll be fine, as long as you remember to focus on the needs of the grieving person by offering help, support, and sympathy—keeping in mind that the reason you're all there is to think warmly of the departed. Above all, *don't* try to minimize or explain the death. Here's a quick look at what to say and what not to say:

WHAT TO SAY

"I'm so sorry about your loss."

"He was a great friend."

"Can I bring you dinner Thursday night?"

"She was an extraordinary person."

"Please know that I am thinking of you."

"Your father was an example for us all."

"I'll call you next week to see how you're doing."

WHAT *NOT* TO SAY

"He's in a better place now."

"Did he have life insurance?"

"It's God's will."

"I know how you feel."

"Well, it looks like you're the man of the house now!"

"Call me if there's anything I can do." (Instead, offer something specific.)

Clothing

While black and dark gray are no longer the required attire for a funeral, you should wear something respectful. Men should dress in a dark suit and tie, and women should wear either a suit or a nice dress. You will want to make sure that the style and cut of the dress are appropriate. Something ruffled or with a low neckline might make the wrong statement during a time of mourning.

During the Reception

Following the funeral or memorial service, there will probably be a reception. Some receptions are solemn and sad; others are joyous, celebratory occasions. Whatever the tone, however, the spirit of the occasion is the same—to honor the departed person's life and to remember him or her fondly through shared stories and reminiscences.

In the Months to Come

The grieving doesn't end once the last guest has left the reception. In the days, weeks, and even months after a funeral, you should make a point of checking in on your friend. Be understanding of the life changes that have occurred for her: This is a time when you'll be required to walk a fine line between sympathy and encouragement, so let your friend's state of mind and personality be your guide in how best to help her in the coming year. Your friend will take her own time to grieve, and this process may change daily. By feeling out her mood, you'll be better able to understand where she is in that process.

PART 3

WORK, PAID AND UNPAID

CHAPTER 18

LANDING THE PERFECT JOB

I F YOU'RE LOOKING for a job or you have a job but plan to start looking for a better one soon—which covers just about everyone I know—then this chapter could be the most important one you'll read. Whether your goal is to land a job with a big company or wait on tables until you strike it rich in Hollywood, in order to make it on your own you'll eventually need to find some kind of steady employment.

At first glance, the challenges involved in finding a job can seem almost overwhelming: Where do you begin looking? Whom should you talk to? And if you find an opening you want to apply for, what next?

Fortunately, the process gets a whole lot easier if you break it down into its three key components: finding a job opening to apply for, submitting your application for the position, and (if you make it that far) going through the job interview. If you concentrate on executing each of these steps as well as you can, the rest of your job search will take care of itself.

Ready? Let's get started!

FINDING A JOB TO APPLY FOR

The key here is to be alert and on the case. Any given job opening is going to stay open only for a short time. This means you've got to keep your eyes peeled and your ear to the ground and be prepared to swing into action the minute you hear of an interesting possibility.

There are four main ways of learning about job openings: networking with friends and acquaintances, watching for openings within your own company, searching job postings in the newspaper and online, and job-hunting through an employment agency.

Networking

Networking is really a fancy term for getting the word out to everyone you know—friends, relatives, contacts from other jobs, even casual acquaintances—that you're looking for a job and would appreciate any leads they might be able to supply. Make sure, too, that they have all of your contact information, so that they can easily get in touch with you if something turns up.

If you know what sort of job you're looking for, say so. This will give the other person a better idea of which leads to pass along: "I'm looking to work with an Internet company," or "I'm interested in an entry-level job with a good retailer," or "I'd like to do something in the financial industry." If you aren't sure what kind of work you want to do, this is also okay to mention—but put a positive spin on it: "I've got a lot of different interests, and I'm open to anything at this point."

Example: Let's say Brian wants to get a job with an advertising firm and one of his friends from college, Andrea, has worked at a few. While networking, he told her that he was looking into advertising. A few

INSTANT TIP

W hen you put out the word that you're searching for work, simply say that you're looking for a job and leave it at that. Don't hand your résumé to a contact unless he or she asks for it.

weeks later, she called back saying that X firm is a great one to work for, and that they might have an opening soon. So Brian gets the name and number of the person Andrea is in touch with and calls. When he does, he says (and this is how to properly name-drop): "Hi, this is Brian Wright. I'm calling at the suggestion of Andrea Smith. She informed me that you might have an opening soon . . ."

Want Ads and Online Job Postings

When looking through the want ads, study carefully what they're looking for and be thinking about what skills you have that could match the job descriptions. Then, when writing your cover letter to send in with your résumé, be sure to highlight the various experiences and accomplishments you have that best meet the company's needs.

Some other points to keep in mind:

- If a company lists just an e-mail address as its form of contact, then you know they'll want you to have e-mail, Internet, and computer skills. Don't forget, too, that many companies now post their job listings on Web sites like Monster.com or Mediabistro.com; the Internet is a great place to start looking.

- If a P.O. box number or address appears, you'll be mailing your résumé and cover letter to the company.

— TELEPHONE TIPS FOR JOB SEEKERS —

- **BEST TIME TO CALL:** *11:15 AM:* Most morning meetings are over by then, and it's still too early to be at lunch. *4:00 PM:* Most afternoon meetings are over but it's still too early to have left the office.

- **VOICE MAIL AS A TOOL:** If you call *after hours* you have a good chance of getting directly to a person's *voice mail service.* When you're leaving a message, you might want to mention what wonderful things you've heard about someone. No need to overdo it: "My name is Lizzie Post. My former coworker Sara Miko spoke highly of your advertising agency and its capabilities . . ." will suffice.

- **THE RIGHT ATTITUDE:** Be *friendly and upbeat* every time you call. Remember that whether you're pursuing unreturned calls to a direct party or you're dealing with a receptionist or personal secretary, you need this person's help—and you should *always be grateful* for any time they can give you, even if it's the seventeenth time you've called.

- **MENTION CONTACTS:** If you've been recommended to this person via networking, now is a good time to bring up your contact's name: "Hi, this is Brian Wright. Bob Johnson suggested I get in touch with you."

- If the ad lists a phone number, call and ask who you should send your cover letter and résumé to, and what address to use. Double-check over the phone the correct spellings of both the name and address. Getting these right will make a big difference to the recipient.

- If you answer a job posting on the Internet, you'll be asked to e-mail your résumé and cover letter. These should be e-mailed as separate attachments, accompanied by a brief message thanking the potential employer for his or her consideration.

- Finally, don't be surprised if you don't hear back from the company, especially if you responded to an online posting. Many companies have a policy of replying only to candidates they're interested in pursuing.

YOU ON PAPER

No matter how impressive you are over the phone or in person, your résumé and cover letter are usually what are going to either land you an interview or not. So it's worth taking as much time on them as necessary, in order to get them just right.

Your Résumé

Your résumé is basically a summary of your work experience, your educational background, and any other activities or honors that you think might help you land the job. (Don't list your references on your résumé; instead, wait until they're requested.)

The typical résumé lists your objective—a quick thumbnail of the sort of position you're hoping to fill and what you would bring to it—then goes into your work history, beginning with your current (or most recent) job and working backward from there. For us newly independents who don't have years of work experience under our belts, it often makes sense to list any relevant summer jobs or internships we've had, as well as our full-time work experience. When listing the different jobs you've had, don't just put down the position and the name of the company and leave it at that. Instead, take a sentence or two to spell out your job responsibilities and achievements.

SAMPLE RÉSUMÉ

Claudia Stone
55 Holland Drive
Burlington, VT 05505
(555) 555-5555
e-mail: claudia@ineedajob.com

OBJECTIVE

A full-time position in the art department of an advertising agency, where I can learn all aspects of design and production and be part of a top-flight team; I have extensive experience in fine arts (drawing and painting), graphic design, computerized animation, and video production.

EXPERIENCE

2006 and 2005: Summer Intern, Evergreen Skiwear Company Marketing Department, Burlington, VT

- Aided in developing, designing, and producing ads for print media and local television.
- Came up with the original idea for the award-winning "Snow Wonderful to Wear in Winter" ad campaign.
- Assisted in planning for and purchasing computers and software in order to develop new computer-design capabilities.

2004-2005: Waitstaff, Monsoon Restaurant, Burlington, VT

- Worked full time in the summer and weekends throughout the school year.
- Received "Summer Staff" award for exemplary customer service.

EDUCATION

Graduated in 2007 with a B.A. in studio art from the University of Vermont.

CONTINUED ▶

SUMMARY
Known as a creative, hard-working team player who is good with people. A fast learner who never makes the same mistake twice. Avid painter of acrylics. Was captain of the 2006-2007 UVM women's synchronized swimming team.

One other piece of advice: No fudging on the facts! You never know when a prospective employer might pick up the phone and call your last boss to ask about you or decide to look you up in your online college yearbook.

The résumé on the preceeding page is for someone fresh out of school and new to the full-time employment scene.

Cover Letter

The purpose of a cover letter is to land you a face-to-face interview by explaining to the prospective employer why your talents and experience make you perfect for the job. Type it on good stationery, and hand-sign it in ink. Keep the letter short, and be sure to mention any contacts you have inside the company.

On the following page is a sample cover letter from our recent college grad.

THE REALITY OF IMPRESSIONS

It may not be nice, and it may not even be fair, but first impressions can make or break you. I worked at one restaurant where your application was thrown out if you came in to apply and asked to borrow a

SAMPLE COVER LETTER

June 10, 2007

William Caldwell
Director, Human Resources
On-Target Advertising
505 Madison Avenue
New York, NY 11000

Dear Mr. Caldwell,

I had the pleasure of meeting your art director, Margaret Johnson, at a clambake on Martha's Vineyard last summer. We have stayed in touch since then, and she recently called to suggest that I apply for an entry-level position that has just opened up in her department.

As you can see from my résumé, although I just graduated from the University of Vermont in June, I have extensive experience in a wide variety of art forms. My studio art degree included courses in advertising design and photography. And while I enjoy painting and drawing, I'm also fascinated by computer graphics and video production.

Having spent the past two summers working for the advertising department of Evergreen Skiwear in my home town of Burlington, I already have some experience in advertising design, and I would very much like to be a part of the dynamic team you're building at On-Target!

I will call you in two weeks to see if we can arrange a meeting. You can also reach me by phone at (555) 555-5555.

Thank you very much for your consideration.

Sincerely,
[SIGNATURE]
Claudia Stone

pen. The owners figured that all good servers keep a pen handy at all times.

You may be asking: *Whatever happened to job skills, work ethic, and references?* Don't get me wrong—these are all important elements of the whole package; but whether or not you get the job rests largely with what happens when you come face-to-face with a potential employer. This is where your *people skills* come into play. Bottom line: Your people skills are often the determining factor in whether you get the job or not.

Sizing Up: The Job Interview

What's the interview really about? To see if you fit into the company. Sure, they want to know if you have the skills to do the work. But that's information you've already given them in your résumé. The interview is a chance for you and the company to meet, and when you do they'll be sizing you up to see if you mesh well with their organization.

How you conduct yourself in the interview will say a lot about the type of person you are: "Mumbles" and "Meek" aren't going to get paid internships at the firm if the interviewer doesn't feel clients will be able to understand what they are saying. And don't forget—this is your chance to size up the company as well.

Dress Up a Notch

I would love to tell you that we live in a nonjudgmental world, but it's simply not the case. Some managers may be able to look past what you wear—but others won't.

A friend of mine was excited by the prospect of a job at a gallery. She went to apply on a hot and humid day, wearing a short skirt, a cute tank top, and a pair of slides. Although she was an art history major with solid credentials, she was dressed as if she was going to the beach rather than to a job interview. She didn't get the job.

The real reason for *dressing up a notch* is that you want the interviewer to focus on *you*, not your clothes. If the interviewer's attention turns to your clothes, you're probably wearing the wrong thing. Here are some ideas for what to wear when job hunting:

MEN	WOMEN
On top: A sport jacket or blazer, with a button-down shirt and tie or polo shirt	**On top:** A button-down shirt, sweater top, or suit jacket
On bottom: Khakis or dark pants, possibly linen pants in summer	**On bottom:** A skirt or dress pants; possibly nice Capri pants
On feet: Stay away from sandals	**On feet:** Closed-toe shoes preferable; if open-toe, aim for conservative style
On face: Clean shaven, no stubble; if you have facial hair, keep it trimmed nicely	**On face:** Go easy on makeup; applying natural colors lightly is better than loading on something striking
Hairstyle: Clean, brushed, and not loaded with gel; if you have dreads, pull them back or keep them neat	**Hairstyle:** Clean, brushed, and out of your face; even a small clip or band will keep it out of your eyes if you want to wear it down
Wrinkle free: Iron your outfit	**Wrinkle free:** Iron your outfit

Try to scope out the place before you go to apply or interview. If you are applying at a trendy café, for example, where it looks as if the staff wears whatever they want (within reason!), showing up in decent jeans and a cool top probably won't hurt your chances. If you're interviewing for a job at an investment bank, however, you'll want to wear a

I'M SORRY—IS THAT YOUR TONGUE RING CLICKING?

In some companies, piercings or tattoos are okay; in others they aren't. This is another reason why the pre-interview snooping mission (or calling up a company's human resources department) is a good idea. In most cases, though, your best bet is to leave the piercing jewelry at home and cover the tattoos. The fact of the matter is, they can be distracting—which is the last thing you want right now. The focus should be on you, not your body art. Remember: You're not trying to make a personal statement; you're trying to get the job.

suit. Applying to be a summer lifeguard? Crisp linen pants and a polo shirt will do the trick.

If you live too far away to visit, simply call the human resources department or a receptionist. You don't even have to identify yourself: "Hi, I'm planning on interviewing with your company, and just wanted to know what your dress policy is."

Six Simple Ways to Make a Good Impression

Your social skills will be of key importance during your interview. Here are six things you can do before and during your interview that will showcase your professionalism:

- **Shake hands** when you introduce yourself. Use a firm grip and actually shake two or three times.

- **Sit down** only after your interviewer invites you to do so.

- *Stand up* when anyone is introduced to you. If someone pops in to drop a message on the interviewer's desk, don't worry about it. But if the interviewer says, "Oh, this is so and so," stand, shake hands, and introduce yourself if the interviewer doesn't do so first.

- *Say, "Thank you."* Right off the bat, this lets the interviewer know that you appreciate their taking the time to meet with you. (You'll do this at the end of the interview as well; see "Say 'Thank You' Again—Then Write It," page 253.)

- *Speak clearly and make eye contact.* Remember "Mumbles" and the job she didn't get? Speaking clearly does two things: it shows you're articulate and it conveys confidence. Making eye contact during the conversation indicates that you are paying attention and that you are seeking engagement with the interviewer.

- *Smile* during the interview; the employer will see that you are inviting and friendly, confident but not cocky, and able to be relaxed and personable in a potentially intimidating situation.

Be Prepared

Even if you've already sent in your résumé, bring with you another copy of your résumé and your application, as well as any portfolio or work samples that you want to showcase. Be ready to talk about your abilities and achievements as well. Much of the interview will obviously consist of the interviewer asking you questions in order to get to know you and your work experience better. Depending on the job, these might range from questions about your previous jobs and educational experience to discussing what you feel you have to offer the company and what your professional goals are.

During the interview, just remember to give straightforward, honest answers. Pumping yourself up and implying you have skills and experience that you don't will only lead to trouble later on. This is also your potential employer's chance to find out what you're like as a person and how well you fit in with the office—so be prepared to talk about topics in your life not directly related to work, such as your interests or hobbies.

Asking Questions

The job interview is also your chance to find out more about the company and decide if you really want to work there. So make a point of learning in advance as much as you can about the company and its policies. That way you'll be better prepared to accept or reject a job offer.

Here are some questions you'll want to consider asking.

- What are the responsibilities of this position?

- What does the job pay? (This one seems obvious, but you'd be surprised at how many people fail to talk money until after they've already more or less accepted the job.)

- What are the chances for advancement?

- What are the benefits? (This is essential information for you to consider.)

- What is the policy for sick days and vacation? (It may seem presumptuous to ask, but if you're going to get only one week of paid vacation a year, wouldn't you rather know before you take the job?)

If you're applying for a summer or part-time job, you'll also want to ask about some additional specifics, such as:

- What days of the week are the busiest (and thus most difficult to take off)?

- Are there certain days when all staff is required to be available?

- How far in advance do employees receive the work schedule?

- What is the pay schedule?

- What is the policy if you schedule me for a day I can't come in?

At the end of the interview, the interviewer will probably ask if you have any additional questions. Here are three things you might want to ask:

- ***Could we take a few minutes to review my résumé?*** If you feel your résumé hasn't gotten sufficient attention, this will give you the chance to make sure the interviewer has reviewed it and to point out any items you want to highlight.

- ***Which of the job's responsibilities are most important?*** By asking this, you'll learn what's most important about the job, demonstrate you're serious about wanting it, and show that you're prepared to ask questions and learn.

- ***What are the company's strengths?*** Asking the interviewer's opinions on the strengths of the company—and then reacting with your own observations—shows that you've researched the company and that you're eager to seek out the opinions of a potential boss.

～ HEADS UP: OUT OF BOUNDS ～

A ccording to the Equal Employment Opportunity Act, there are certain questions an employer is not allowed to ask during an interview:

- How old are you?
- Where were you born?
- Are you married and/or do you have children?
- What is your sexual orientation?
- What religion are you?

If you *are* asked one of these questions, you'll have to decide whether you want to answer it. You can always say something like, "I'm sorry, I'm not required to answer that question by law." If you do, however, you may jeopardize your chances of getting the job. Another approach is to dodge the question by countering it with a question of your own: "I'm surprised by that question—could you explain what it has to do with my getting this job?" This gives the interviewer a chance to rethink (and hopefully retract) the question.

Say "Thank You" Again—Then Write It

When the interview is concluded, be sure to thank the interviewer once again for taking the time to meet with you. Then, after you get home, follow up with a thank-you note. Keep it short and simple— three or four lines will do—and make sure it's absolutely error-free.

For example:

Dear Mr. Hathaway,

Thank you for taking the time to interview me on Thursday, June 14. It was my pleasure to meet with you and see the establishment. I am very interested in the possibility of working with you, and I look forward to hearing from you.

Sincerely,
Jacqueline F. Huette

Persistence Pays Off

After you send in your résumé, it's perfectly okay to call the company and check on your application—just don't do it the very next day. Unless you're given a specific time frame for the company's decision, two weeks is an appropriate amount of time to wait before calling.

If you've made it to the interview stage, try to pin down an actual "hear back" date, when you can expect to hear from the company. Once that date arrives, the general rule of thumb is: "One day after." If they say, "We'll call you next Tuesday," but they don't, then give them a call on Wednesday. Believe me: You're not being pushy—just persistent.

CHAPTER 19

ON THE JOB

OU'VE SURVIVED the application mill, made it through the interview process, and landed the job of your dreams: Now it's time to get to work.

THE FIRST DAY

It may sound like a cliché, but this is a big day. Day 1 is impression day—the day that coworkers and bosses will get their real first sense of you and how you work in their environment. Today's the day to get everything right—which is why the following are absolute musts:

THE THREE KEYS TO JOB SUCCESS

- Don't be late
- Be prepared
- Dress for the job you want, not the job you have

Be on Time

It is of the utmost importance that today, of all days, you *show up on time*. Set your alarm early—set two alarms if necessary—and make sure that you have more than enough time to get showered, dressed, and ready and to get yourself to work a few minutes early, leaving enough time to grab a cup of coffee and a paper at the corner store if you want to. Traffic can sometimes be a legitimate excuse for lateness, but even the excuse of a delayed train won't fly today. Show your boss right at the start that you can get to the office on time.

Be Prepared

Be ready to start digging in and working that day. While the first day is often spent learning where things are and who's who at the office, you also want to be prepared for any assignment they might throw at you.

INTRODUCE YOURSELF

In your first few days at work, be sure to introduce yourself to all the people you work with. If you bump into someone you don't know and it's a good time to chat for a minute, walk up and say something like, "Hi, I'm Ben. I just started in the marketing department this week." The other person will then introduce himself and most likely welcome you to the company. Don't worry about appearing overly eager: Most coworkers will be pleased that you tactfully made the first move and glad to know they have such a sociable new colleague to work with.

Ask Questions

Ask your coworkers where supplies are kept, how to use the office copier and other equipment, and which employees are go-to people. And don't be shy about asking for help if you need it. Everyone was a new employee once, and people are glad to help. Besides, it's a good way to get to know your coworkers better.

Not a Lunch Date Day

If your new coworkers want to take you out for a get-acquainted lunch, fine—but today is not the day to meet a friend for a leisurely bite.

Keep Your Cell Phone Turned Off

Friends can always leave messages if they need to. Today you don't want that little phone ringing while you're being introduced to the boss or when projects are being explained to you.

Dress Up a Notch

Today you want no wardrobe fouls, so wear crisp, clean clothing that is not only job-appropriate but also a shade dressier than what you'd or-dinarily wear to the office.

CUBICLE AND SHARED-OFFICE ETIQUETTE

Working in a cubicle or a shared office might not be your favorite thing to do, but in today's cost-conscious business world, offices where workers share a room or sit side by side in cubicles are here to stay.

When you're working in close quarters, good office etiquette becomes critically important. Here are a few things to bear in mind when personal space is tight:

- Just because there's no door between you and your coworkers does *not* mean you can visit anybody anytime you want. People simply can't get their work done if someone keeps dropping by every five minutes or (if you share a space) turning to tell you their latest thought. *Always* ask someone if they have a minute to speak before breaking into their space to ask a question.

- When working in cubicles, volume control is essential. Whether you're speaking with a coworker or you're on the phone with someone, be conscious of keeping your voice at a reasonable level. This goes double if you share an office with someone.

- When you have a question for a coworker a few cubicles away, don't shout it out to them. If it's too much trouble to walk over and talk face-to-face, pick up the phone and call.

- If you work in a cubicle or shared office and you need to make or take a private call, either go to an empty office or conference room or call back on your own time.

- Keep fidgets to a minimum. Drumming your fingers, tapping your foot or a pen, whistling, humming, cracking your knuckles . . . there are a million little noises that get noticed when people are trying to concentrate. Put them with thirty other people's little noises, and you've got one noisy, open-floor office. Even one annoying sound can be the death of an otherwise productive silence. So try to keep those noises in check.

- If you listen to music on your computer or iPod, use headphones wherever possible. If headphones aren't allowed, keep the volume low, and check to make sure it's not bothering anyone. Same goes for the chirps, beeps, and other sounds your computer is programmed to make.

COPIER MACHINE ETIQUETTE

Ah, the copier machine: always being used by someone else to print out *War and Peace* when you have a rush job to do—when it's not busy breaking down at the worst possible moment. To keep things cool in this notorious office hot spot, here are some general copier guidelines:

- When you have a big job to do, check to see if anyone else has a small one they need to get done. If so, let them use the machine first.

- Always check the paper drawer after completing a large copying run, and refill it if the supply is low.

INSTANT TIP

If you're looking for a new job, do not—repeat, *do not*—use the office machine to copy your résumé or cover letters. There are way too many stories of people who forgot and left their résumé in the copier, only to find themselves leaving their current employer a little sooner than planned.

ASK LIZZIE: THE ANNOYING COWORKER

Q: One of my coworkers has a habit of clearing his throat loudly every few minutes. It drives me crazy, but at the same time I feel funny complaining about something so trivial. What should I do?

LIZZIE: One reality of any job is that your coworkers aren't necessarily going to be people you would choose to hang out with. In light of this fact, you're going to have to decide whether the little things they do that bug you are really worth a confrontation. (And don't forget, someone may be itching to fix one of your "little things" as well.)

How can you tell if an annoyance is worth confronting someone about? First, ask yourself how bothersome the annoyance really is. If it's truly affecting your work, then you need to have a discreet talk with your coworker. There's no need to embarrass him—just explain what's bothering you and that you want to work together to find a solution: "I'm sorry, Charlotte, but your radio is really making it hard for me to concentrate on this report. Do you think you could turn it down or listen through headphones? Thanks; I really appreciate it."

If the behavior still doesn't change, you may want to ask your boss to tackle the subject. Alternatively, if you know other employees are bothered by it as well, you might want to approach your boss as a group. This will make it look less like you are attacking this person and more like an issue that others have a problem with, too.

- Take responsibility for adding toner when necessary, and for contacting whoever maintains the machine if there's a breakdown or other servicing is needed.

- If you have to do any large personal copying job, take it to a print store rather than doing it at your office.

- If someone leaves a document in the copier, resist the urge to read it. Instead, glance at it just enough to see who it belongs to, then return it promptly to its owner.

FAX ETIQUETTE

Fax etiquette is pretty simple:

- Use a cover sheet.

- Remember that nothing sent by fax is truly private. Something may be marked confidential on a cover sheet, but whoever handles the fax can always read it if they choose to, even if it *is* bad office etiquette.

- Number the pages of the document and state the total on the cover sheet.

- If the fax is long, call first and let the recipient know that it might take a while for the fax to be transmitted. Also, check around the office before sending it, to make sure no one else has any high-priority faxes to send.

- Don't send personal faxes unless the company approves of the practice.

- If you discover a fax that just arrived, either deliver it to the recipient or let him or her know it's here.

PHONE ETIQUETTE

"Good afternoon, the Emily Post Institute, this is Lizzie. How can I help you?" That's my standard greeting when I answer the phone at the EPI offices. It's important when you are answering phones for a company to use an upbeat, cheerful voice—one that immediately lets the caller know you're ready and willing to help. Your company may have a specific greeting they want you to use, or they may leave it up to you to say what you like. Either way, you should always answer the phone using either your name or the company name or both; that way, the caller knows they've reached the right place.

Whenever you take a message for someone else, be sure to write down

- The date

- The time

- The name of the person calling

- How this person can be reached

- Any message the caller wishes to leave

Add your initials or name to the message, so the person who is out will know who took it. For example: "Chris: John Halbert of Paint-It-Now Art Supplies called, 9/13 at 11:15 AM. Wanted to know how many boxes of size 8 fan brushes are needed. Call back when you get the chance: 1-800-555-9807. LP"

AT THE PUSH OF A BUTTON: INTERNET AND E-MAIL ETIQUETTE

When it comes to using the Internet at work, there's one thing above all you should be aware of: If you use a company-owned computer, your management has the ability and the legal right to review every Web site you've visited. So leave personal Web-surfing for your home computer and stick to work-related searches at the office.

Remember, too, that your e-mails are also open to scrutiny. Not only can your company look at the content of your office e-mails anytime they wish but also any e-mail can be forwarded to the rest of the office and beyond at the push of a button. Don't e-mail any message that you aren't willing to see broadcast to the world. If you have something confidential to discuss, do it in person or over the phone—or mail or messenger a hard copy of the communication.

SMALL-TALK SKILLS

Small talk helps build your relationships at work. It's what lets the other guys know you're human. While pretty much any topic is up for grabs, avoid talking about issues that are too personal; discussions of sex, relationships, religion, politics, medical conditions, and drinking or substance abuse all have potential to go too far for office chat—and could find you at the center of some rumors.

Some other conversational tips worth keeping in mind at work:

- Before stopping to chat with a coworker, gauge whether the person really has the time. If it's not a good time for the other person, don't be offended—just say, "Oh, sorry, we'll talk later."

- Don't dominate the conversation; leave room for the other person to respond and show interest in their opinions and ideas.

- Include other colleagues in your conversation if they come along and seem interested.

- Keep up with world news, local news, and entertainment and sports news; they are all great conversation starters.

- To end a conversation, excuse yourself once someone has stated a concluding thought. If you have to go in the middle of a conversation, say something like "I have to get back to that page layout now, but let's talk about this over coffee tomorrow."

WHEN THE GLOVES COME OFF

It's inevitable that differences of opinion between coworkers will occur from time to time. When this happens, the key is not to let the disagreement become personal. The moment you start saying anything snippy or rude such as "idiot" or "jerk," you've overstepped the bounds of professionalism.

Here are three bits of advice that can come in handy during any argument:

- ***Stick to the subject at hand.*** Referring to old issues, bringing up someone's personal life, or tallying up who's won previous

DID YOU HEAR THE
NEWS ABOUT . . . ?

ossip and rumors can be pretty dangerous in the workplace. Since we newly independents are often "on the floor" with our coworkers and bosses, gossip is easily overheard—and even if you're discreet about it, murmurs can spread like wildfire through an office. We all want to be on good terms with our coworkers, and in an effort to get closer we often put our cards on the table. It's up to you to choose how much to reveal to your coworkers about your lifestyle and your relationships.

If you find out others are gossiping about your personal life, you can decide whether to let it roll off your back or to set some mouths straight. When it comes to your professional life, however, you need to confront the rumors head-on: "I heard you've been telling people that Mr. Jones and I have something going on. We don't. And you need to be clear on that, because my work reputation is on the line. I need you to stop spreading this rumor and inform whoever you've told it to that what you said isn't true."

---

arguments will only sidetrack you and prevent you from solving the problem in front of you. If Jim says something like, "And by the way, you never even counted the inventory that time in January," simply steer the conversation back to the current topic: "Jim, we've both made mistakes in the past. Right now, we're trying to solve this dilemma."

- *Be open to compromise.* When a debate occurs at work, there's rarely a clear-cut right or wrong answer. So be willing to negotiate a little and be ready to accept the fact that a good compromise may be as close as you'll get to your desired solution.

- *Bag the brag.* It's always nice to be proven right, but rubbing it in by saying "I told you so" will only make you look childish. If you *were* right, your coworkers will recognize this without your announcing it.

GIVE HELP TO GET THE JOB DONE

It's perfectly all right to ask for or give help wherever you work. The trick is to give help only when you can and ask for it only when you really need it.

It's the little things that we can team up on to get the job done that make a difference to our coworkers. The more serious the jobs get, the more the help is appreciated. Not every favor will be returned, nor should you be expecting this or keeping a mental tally of who "owes" you. If that's the way you think, you're going to be sorely disappointed on numerous occasions. Instead, realize that you're helping the whole business run better; you're part of a team, and teammates help each other out.

THE FRO-WORKER: WHEN FRIENDS ARE COWORKERS

There's a difference between coworkers who become friends and friends who become coworkers. It's easier to maintain a professional aspect to your relationship when a coworker becomes a good friend. Sure, you may swap jokes while you're putting together press kits—but here's a reason that office parties have the word *office* in their name. They're parties, yes—but they're business, too. Whatever you may have heard, this is not a time to hit on a cute coworker, or cut loose and end up with the proverbial lampshade on your head. It's okay to engage in personal conversation and get to know your coworkers better; just don't do anything that will make it to the watercooler the next day.

your friendship is based on an initial understanding that you're both at work and that you can snap into your professional selves as needed.

When you start working with someone who is already a good friend, on the other hand, you'll have to make an effort to switch into work mode when the two of you are on the job. This isn't always easy, but it may help to recall that you both have bills to pay and want cash to go out and have fun with; ergo, you both want to keep your jobs—which also means keeping the friendship within professional limits at the office. You can be chummy, playful, and helpful with each other, but remember: Business comes first.

After hours, of course, it's a different story. Still, when socializing with friends from work, always remember that what happens tonight could get talked about tomorrow morning. So keep this in mind when you're deciding whether to order that extra drink or share that delicious gossip about the coworker down the hall.

THE HEAD HONCHO

Some of my bosses have been wonderful—giving advice, praising when praise was due, encouraging the staff, and looking out for our ven when things get tense at work and tempers are flaring, re-member to respect your boss. She's most likely someone you can learn from. More important, she's the one who holds the key to your paycheck, as well as references for future jobs or promotions.

well-being. Others have been less than wonderful—designating a scape-goat, promising promotions that never came, and (my personal favorite) telling you only half of what you were supposed to do, then yelling at you for not completing the other half.

Still, whether they're good or bad bosses (or managers or owners or whatever title they go by), our superiors are people, too. Most of our bosses will do weird or annoying things at times or will impose at least some rules that we think are ridiculous. We need to do our best to understand and respect them. So take the time to get to know your boss and see where the relationship takes you. And remember, he or she won't be your boss forever.

On the other hand, remember, too, that people don't change radi-cally overnight. If you're unlucky enough to get a boss who's a really bad boss—someone who's disrespectful to her employees, doesn't look out for her staff, or doesn't have the company's interests in mind—you have two options: you can stay and zip your lips about any complaints you've got or you can leave and find a job with a boss who *does* care about treating his colleagues and company with consideration.

CHAPTER 20

WHEN SCHOOL IS YOUR JOB

ISN'T IT GREAT?! You're in college, you've got roommates you're not related to, party after party to hit up, no curfew, and you have class only three days a week . . . class . . . oh, no—CLASS!

Yes, college is about many things, and in terms of etiquette I certainly didn't want to skip class. Because no matter how much fun school may be, you're there to get an education that will be the launching pad for your adult career. And etiquette (you guessed it!) can help—particularly in how you deal with your professors and your course work.

CLASSROOM ETIQUETTE

How you handle yourself in class can't help but influence how your professor views your attitude toward his or her course—and, by extension, how your performance is evaluated. Here are some general guidelines to follow in any classroom:

Be on Time

There is nothing more distracting to a professor and your fellow students than to watch helplessly as 10, 15, 20 students waltz in late for a lecture. If you have a schedule conflict—your previous class is all the way on the other side of campus, for example, and it really does take longer than usual to get to this class—talk with your professor about it. That way, she'll know to expect a slight interruption near the start of each class and be able to adjust to it.

Introduce Yourself

Whether you're in a class of 15 students or 150, always make a point of introducing yourself to your professor at the start of every course. This is also a good time to bring up any questions or special requests you might have.

This face-to-face introduction will bookmark you in your professor's memory and lay the groundwork for developing a relationship. If you run into difficulty in the class, you'll be able to go to her for help without it looking like a last-minute attempt to salvage your final grade. Plus, you never know when a recommendation will come in handy. Professors remember students who care enough to make the effort to connect.

Eating in Class

When classes are scheduled tightly, we don't always have time to sit down and eat food outside of class, so many of us just bring something with us to class. I've rarely run across a professor who has a problem with this, *provided you eat your food discreetly.* If possible, it's always a good idea to bring foods that can be eaten quietly. Something like a banana or an orange, which doesn't have a wrapper, is ideal.

I f you know you're going to have to leave a class early for some reason, let your professor know at the start of class. Then when the time comes, simply get out of your seat and leave the room *quietly*. (Ditto if you have to use the restroom.) If the classroom door is shut, open and close it as softly as you can. The idea here is to be noticed as little as possible.

Oh yeah—and if you bring a drink with you, *don't* slurp those last few drops through your straw. If you're so desperate for that last precious liquid, remove the top and drink it down.

THE IMPORTANCE OF SETTING PRIORITIES

During my freshman year of college, I had to take a required art history course with a professor known for his intellectual brilliance. At the start of the first class, he announced: "Last semester I had one hundred forty-eight students. Only twenty of them received an A, and I am not afraid to fail you." Great opening line, right? But he also offered us some superb advice: "I understand that for many of you this is a distribution requirement. And at this level of education and independence, you need to consider what your priorities are. If you have other tests and papers that are more important than this class, then by all means spend more time on them. Don't come crying to me, however, when you get a C in my class. You have to decide whether to make my class a high priority or a lesser priority, then accept your decision."

I thought this pronouncement sounded pretty bleak when I first heard it. But after thinking about it for a week, I found that his words made me much more relaxed in his class. I realized that he was right—it was okay to have priorities. I just needed to learn that I wasn't necessarily going to get straight As in everything. I put serious effort into that class, but I never let it overwhelm my other studies, and I never felt bad about it.

That professor was absolutely right: Lose the guilt; accept the grade. You don't have to be a "wonder student" in every course. Your goal isn't perfection, or to win the professor's undying admiration—you're just trying to balance your responsibilities and get the best education you can.

ASKING FOR HELP

If you're in jeopardy of getting a low grade in one of your classes or you've fallen behind and are totally screwed for a paper or exam or some other assignment, I have two words for you: *Seek help!* All teachers have office hours. Simply go at the appointed time, wait your turn if necessary, and then spell out your problem, concisely and without elaboration: "I just can't seem to get started on my term paper and I'm getting worried, since it's due in a month."

I can't tell you what a difference this will make, even with the strictest of professors. If you're writing a paper, your professor can point you in the right direction and might even help brainstorm ideas with you. If a test is coming up, she can suggest the areas that you'll need to study. But none of this will ever happen unless you *seek help.*

GETTING THE GRADE
YOU DESERVE

I had a real learning experience during my junior year in college. I was having difficulty in a class that I really enjoyed: My final research paper came back with all sorts of positive comments scrawled on it—

GROUP PROJECTS

When your professor assigns a group project, your course work is no longer just about you. To get a good grade, you'll have to coordinate with other people, put in your share of time and effort, and be able to show your professor that you pulled your weight.

To make sure a group project goes smoothly:

- Make every effort to schedule meetings when everyone can make it.

- If you're going to miss a meeting or know you're going to be late, let someone in the group know in advance so they won't be waiting around for you to show up. Then schedule a time with one of the group members to catch up on what you missed.

- When you commit to working on a certain part of the project, live up to that commitment. Remember, the other group members are counting on you.

- If you find you're having trouble with your part of the assignment, don't suffer in silence. Instead, tell your colleagues as soon as possible and ask for their help.

"Great connection," "Yes!" "His work did reflect this," "Good job"—and then the grade: a big, fat red F. The reason she failed me was that I'd used the wrong style in my citations, and had referenced class notes without citing them.

I was devastated. It had been a trying semester, and all I wanted to do was throw in the towel—but I couldn't, because it was a required class and I needed at least a C to get course credit. So I called my advisor and asked to meet with her. When we sat down together, she gave me some really great advice. "Whatever you do, don't whine to your professor. It may have been a difficult semester for you, but what really matters is that you're putting effort into this class that isn't being reflected in your grades. I think you should go talk to your professor. You need to work *with* her to find a way for your final grade to reflect your effort. You may not get the F changed, and you still may not make a C in the end, but at least you'll have communicated about it. And if you fail the class, you can always try again."

With new confidence I dressed up a notch and went to meet with the professor. She started by explaining to me that she couldn't change the grade on my paper. I could feel the tears welling up, even though I didn't want them to. We talked about how good the paper was and the fact that my mistakes were only technical, but that technical stuff can be very important. I told her that I felt a little gypped because I'd spoken up in class and seemed to be right on track and yet I was heading for a low average in the course.

Finally, I explained to her that I really needed this grade, because if I didn't get a C, I wouldn't get credit for the course. She laughed and said, "Of course you can still pull off a C!" My eyes were the size of golf balls and I started to cry a little.

"Really?" I said. "Thank God, because I was so scared. This course has been so hard for me, even though I enjoy it, and I just couldn't bear taking the class over again." My tears made her cry a little, too. "It'll be hard, because you'll have to get an A on the final, but I know you have the knowledge to do it. And Lizzie, even if you don't get a C,

I can write a letter to the department saying that you got below a C only on a technicality and that you really know the course content." I hadn't known a professor could do that! "I'm glad you came and talked to me," she added.

The bottom line: Mistakes happen—and it's up to you to try and fix them, before they turn into festering problems. So communicate with your professors. It makes all the difference in the world.

By the way, I did get my C.

INDEX

EMILY POST 1872 TO 1960

EMILY POST began her career as a writer at the age of thirty-one. Her romantic stories of European and American society were serialized in *Vanity Fair, Collier's, McCall's,* and other popular magazines. Many were also successfully published in book form.

Upon its publication in 1922, her book, *Etiquette,* topped the nonfiction best-seller list, and the phrase "according to Emily Post" soon entered our language as the last word on the subject of social conduct. Mrs. Post, who as a girl had been told that well-bred women should not work, was suddenly a pioneering American woman. Her numerous books, a syndicated newspaper column, and a regular network radio program made Emily Post a figure of national stature and importance throughout the rest of her life.

Good manners reflect something from inside—an innate sense of consideration for others and respect for self.
—*Emily Post*

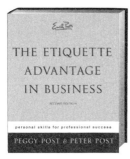